Firmly Convinced

Readers are encouraged to go to www.MissionPointPress.com to contact the author, or to contact the publisher about how to buy this book in bulk at a discounted rate.

Published by Mission Point Press
2554 Chandler Rd.
Traverse City, MI 49696
(231) 421-9513
www.MissionPointPress.com

ISBN:
Hardcover: 978-1-961302-89-1
Softcover: 978-1-961302-90-7

Library of Congress Control Number: 2024915979

Printed in the United States of America

FIRMLY CONVINCED

By Chet Wiech

MISSION POINT PRESS

This book is dedicated to my sister Gloria Bondrow. She was the best big sister a guy could ever be blessed with. She passed just months before FIRMLY CONVINCED went to print, and I can only hope that somehow her kindness, compassion and humor she taught me are reflected in these pages. Love you, Sis.

TABLE OF CONTENTS

FIRMLY CONVINCED

A revealing look at the criminal justice system through the eyes of a career prosecutor

Written by: Chief Assistant Atlantic County
New Jersey Prosecutor Chet Wiech, Retired

A GLOSSARY OF TERMS

(in some instances according to Oxford Languages)

Victim, noun, a person harmed or killed as the result of a crime.

Defendant, noun, the accused in a court of law; an individual who often causes harm to, ruins, or even ends a person's life.

Prosecutor, noun, a lawyer who institutes legal proceedings against someone; a lawyer who conducts the case against a defendant in a criminal case.

Conviction, noun, a formal declaration that someone is guilty of criminal offense, made by the verdict of a jury, or the decision of a judge in a court of law.

Judge, noun, sometimes another obstacle to a conviction.

With these simple definitions in mind, you are now ready to begin reading.

AN INTRODUCTION

I WAS NEVER ONE OF those people whose entire life's purpose was to become a lawyer. Attending law school was essentially my fallback option. With that in mind, it may be surprising to learn that I proudly spent twenty-five years as a prosecutor, years that, while difficult, I wouldn't exchange for anything. Let's rewind a bit to get the full picture.

Formal education did not appeal to me at all in high school. If it wasn't for playing sports, making friends, and partying, those three years may have been a complete waste of time. My high school teachers were very good for the most part. I simply didn't apply myself.

Realizing I was not college material, I enlisted in the U.S. Navy before graduating from high school. I wanted to be sure I made the right choice, so the summer after graduation I took a factory job. My grandfathers, dad, and uncles all worked at different factory jobs, and I needed to see if I was capable of continuing the legacy. I was not. The work was extremely hard and dangerous.

The four years I spent in the military gave me time to think about my future. From the deck of a Navy destroyer, a college education now appeared to be a very good idea. Especially since I could use the G.I. Bill to pay for it.

This was the beginning of the serious part of my life. I was honorably discharged from the Navy, got married, and began college in the same year. This year my wife and I will celebrate forty-seven years together.

I attended John Jay College of Criminal Justice for my first three semesters. John Jay was a member college in the City University of New York, a group of colleges once referred to as the poor man's Harvard. The faculty there was exceptional and eclectic. I had an avowed Marxist for Political Theory and a rabbi for Philosophy, who was the New York City Police Chaplain at the time.

I then transferred to Fordham University. My thought was that Fordham's name recognition would give me a better chance of getting into graduate school. Fordham was much more conservative than John Jay, but it did provide excellent opportunities. My senior year I had an internship at the United Nations. I graduated cum laude from Fordham with a double major in Economics and Political Science.

New York University offered a master's program in public administration that I was interested in. But it was mathematics intensive. I felt that might be a struggle since I had taken a limited number of college math courses. Therefore, law school became my default position. I took the LSAT exam, scored well, and was accepted into Seton Hall University Law School.

I took every criminal and trial advocacy course offered. Unlike many of my classmates, I got involved in clinical programs, especially those which provided opportunities for court appearances. As a law student, I got my ass handed to me more than once by a judge, but those humbling experiences fueled my desire to become a trial lawyer.

My first paying job as a lawyer was with Legal Services in Newark, New Jersey. I was a staff attorney in the Housing Unit where I spent every day in court representing indigent defendants in landlord/tenant actions. My next job was as an associate attorney in a small firm in East Orange, New Jersey. While I hated the job, it provided me with an opportunity to represent defendants in both municipal and criminal court matters. In fact, it is where I had my first criminal jury trial. I still feel that the prosecutor's arrogance and short-sightedness in that case contributed to my client's acquittal. That started me pursuing a career as a prosecutor. The citizens of New Jersey were entitled to better representation.

When I drove down to the Atlantic City area to interview with the Atlantic County Prosecutor's Office, I did not think I would get the job. I didn't know a soul in Atlantic County and felt my lack of a "hook" foreclosed my chances. At least that is the way things worked in North Jersey, which is why I was driving two hours south for the interview.

I had already been offered a job with the New Jersey attorney general in Trenton, but the assistant prosecutor position in Atlantic City would eventually provide me with the criminal trial work I desired. The interview went well, and much to my amazement, it was advantageous not to have a "hook," as the prosecutor wanted lawyers beholden to no one.

Two weeks later, I was offered the job as an assistant Atlantic County prosecutor. I readily accepted, and since the offer was conditioned on my starting a month earlier than was originally negotiated, I drove two hours each way for the first month of work.

I started as an assistant prosecutor preparing and presenting cases to grand juries. I retired eleven years ago as chief assistant prosecutor in charge of the Trial Section. My twenty-five years of service included over two hundred jury trials.

Writing about my experiences was something I kicked around for years. I did not want the book to only be a personal memoir, and I wanted to write about the truth. These vignettes describe events that really occurred. No facts have been added to sensationalize them.

I nearly abandoned authoring this book halfway through. Someone whose opinion I respect challenged me by asking what I envisioned the book becoming. He asked me whether I was writing about my career taking me from being idealistic to jaded, an incident of malfeasance, or an injustice or public corruption I felt driven to expose. None of those things drove me to write and, fearing it lacked sufficient salacious and unsavory material, I became worried that no one would care to read the book.

What I hope the reader gains from this book is a better understanding of the complexity of the criminal justice system attributed to its many participants, all of whom happen to be human. I also hope to help the reader comprehend the weight placed upon those dedicated to preserving the rule of law, which, simply stated, means that we are a country of laws, not men.

At a time when people of wealth ignore the rule of law, often in the interest of acquiring power, the battle fought by current and future prosecutors to maintain it will be greater than any challenge faced in a solitary case or courtroom. That battle has always existed but has become magnified (or magafied).

The criminal justice system is imperfect, but if the rule of law is compromised, the ensuing result will be tyranny and chaos. The criminal justice system is also very demanding on all its participants. Prosecutors need to understand the importance of perfecting their craft to maintain a process perceived to be fair and just for both victims and those accused of committing crimes. Defense counsel need to ensure that their clients' Constitutional rights are protected, and that the accused receive a process which appears objectively fair. Judges wield great power and need to adjudicate the rules and laws fairly, and most importantly, apolitically.

While authoring this book was cathartic for me, helping me recall how much work—and at times, fun—my career as a prosecutor was, I fear that rising criticism and cynicism about the criminal justice system will dissuade good people from continuing the battle.

Anyone choosing to take on the job of prosecutor must do it for all the right reasons. Seeking the position to acquire some trial experience and then moving on to a higher paying career in private practice seems to be what motivates many new law school graduates. Of all reasons to become a prose-cutor, that is the worst.

The commitment to the profession needs to be selfless and strong. Career prosecutors need to take on difficult cases to ensure confidence in the system. Anyone who "cherry-picks" the winners to pad their record and stroke their ego only con-tributes to its erosion. My hope is that the prosecutors cur-rently fighting the battle decide to give it their all. If not, I hope they will choose to do something else with their lives.

As you may recall, the first word listed in my glossary of terms was "victim." While a prosecutor's first responsibility is to represent the interest of the citizens in that jurisdiction, the rights and feelings of the victim should never be ignored. In fact, I do not know how one could prosecute a case without being motivated in part by the victim's loss or suffering, and the courage and confidence the victim or the victim's survi-vors place in the prosecutor to seek that which is just.

This is not to say that the victim or the victim's survivors have the last word in a case. They do not; that responsibility falls squarely on the shoulders of the prosecutor. The feelings and opinions of the victim or their survivors should never be ignored. They should always be made to feel that they have some input in the outcome to preserve the integrity of the system.

I am not being self-righteous with these comments. Rather, I am being truthful.

DEFINING "FIRMLY CONVINCED"

ONE OF THE MOST ELUSIVE concepts in law is the idea of "reasonable doubt." And yet, despite being so difficult to define, reasonable doubt is central to prosecutors' work, a challenge they must confront daily in courtrooms throughout the country. Every defendant charged with a criminal offense is presumed innocent unless the prosecutor can prove the defendant's guilt beyond a reasonable doubt. A judge is required to use that term so many times in opening and final jury instructions that it resounds like a blow from a hammer to the prosecutor's head.

In a civil case (one about damages and money), a person seeking redress need only prove by a preponderance of the evidence that the accused caused the harm. Meaning, it is "more likely than not" that the actions of the accused caused the harm. Jury instructions usually quantify this term by using 51% to 49% as an illustration. Administrative proceedings (actions before a government agency) use "clear and convincing evidence" as the standard of proof. The clear and convincing evidence standard requires more proof than a preponderance, but less than in a criminal trial, where guilt must be proven beyond a reasonable doubt.

To make matters worse for the prosecution, a judge in a criminal case is required to instruct jurors on the civil and administrative standards, comparing the types of proof all three require. When the judge is finished, it's now defense counsel's chance to use and convolute the term "reasonable doubt" as many times as possible in opening and closing statements. Especially in cases where little or no defense to the charges exists.

I cannot tell you how many times I saw defense counsel use the railing separating the jury box from the rest of the courtroom to define reasonable doubt. Counsel, in explaining the three standards of proof, would say that on one end of the railing is the preponderance standard, about ninety percent of the way down is clear and convincing, and at the furthest end is reasonable doubt. A pretty stark example, and not truly accurate.

When defense counsel used that argument, I would counter by telling jurors that I had heard that story so many times I finally realized the purpose of the railing: it was there as "a defense prop." The same defense counsel never used the railing example twice in cases we tried together.

Usually, I would "cherry-pick" the jury instructions and focus on the parts most advantageous to the prosecution. Judges are also required to instruct jurors that a reasonable doubt is "not a mere possible or imaginary doubt," but rather an honest and reasonable uncertainty that exists in their minds after giving careful consideration to all the evidence in the case. The jurors are also instructed that if the evidence leaves them "firmly convinced" of the defendant's guilt, they must return a verdict of guilty.

I would tell jurors that since a trial is a search for the truth, they must determine which explanation of the evidence represents the best version of it. That was usually followed by my "Nerf ball" description of what truth is. I would liken truth to a Nerf ball: no matter how it is twisted and reshaped, it will always return to its original form when left alone. While the defense and prosecution each present their own version of the truth, the jury must see past possible distortions to find the real truth supported by the facts.

My experience was that jurors responded best to analogy or example. In discussing reasonable doubt, it was important to explain what reasonable doubt is and is not. Often analogy and example could be used together.

When addressing reasonable doubt, I told jurors that my family looked forward to our annual week of camping in Maine every August, attempting to escape the heat and humidity of South Jersey. We would pack the car, and without fail, we would be ten miles north on our trip up the Garden State Parkway when my wife would ask if we unplugged the Mr. Coffee. Knowing that we would be gone for a week and the house might burn down, we would turn around and go back home to make sure we unplugged it. I would tell the jurors that reasonable doubt caused us to act as we did in that situation.

Conversely, I would give them the same scenario, except this time my wife asks if we turned the furnance off. With the air conditioning running for months in summer, we wouldn't turn around to see if we were wasting money on heating oil because there was no way the furnace would be running. I would tell jurors that this was an example where reasonable doubt did not exist.

If nothing else, I am firmly convinced that a more precise definition of reasonable doubt awaits discovery by some legal scholar. For now, the law requires that perfect not get in the way of good when it comes to defining reasonable doubt.

YOU CAN BE TERMINATED AT ANY TIME

IT WAS A BEAUTIFUL SOUTH Jersey October afternoon as I headed to the courthouse to finish the usual list of sixty or so arraignment and status conference cases. My thoughts were drawn to two things: the Buffalo Bills game on Monday Night Football and retirement. The Bills game was just hours away, so it took precedence. Retirement after twenty-five years as an assistant and now chief assistant Atlantic County prosecutor was still months away.

That day, I was covering for one of the assistant prosecutors I supervised who was out sick. I did not mind having to fill in—the legal matters were something I could handle in my sleep. Plus, being busy in court helped pass the day while beers chilled in my refrigerator and gave me time to contemplate where to order chicken wings from for the game.

As I passed through the metal detectors for the several thousandth time in my career, routinely emptying my pockets, opening my trial bag for inspection, and exchanging

11

pleasantries with Sheriff's Officer Ed, whom I had known for years, my instincts were telling me something was off. My instincts would prove to be correct.

Many years before, when I decided to accept the position of assistant prosecutor, an old and wizened attorney told me that prosecutors held great status within the legal profession. The only caveat, he said, was that after a while judges hated you for mucking up their dockets with trials, defense counsel hated you for forcing them to try cases, defendants naturally hated you because in their minds you were responsible for sending them to prison, and your family would even come to hate you because all the time you devoted to trial took away from time you could have spent with them. My family still loved me after all my years as a prosecutor, but he was right about the others.

With all this hatred constantly swirling around you, and considering that many of the people you encountered were rapists, robbers, child molesters, and murderers, you might ask why anyone in their right mind would become a prosecutor. A fair question, and one I often struggled to answer during my career. It certainly was not the pay, which was dreadfully low in terms of lawyer salaries. It was not prestige, since most of my career was spent in an office housed in trailers so rancid they were eventually condemned. And it wasn't security; on more than one occasion a judge threatened to lock me up for contempt of court. I'm still in search of the answer.

Unbelievably, in the history of the great State of New Jersey, no prosecutor has ever been killed by anyone they prosecuted. Surely, there were several cases that I prosecuted during which I received veiled or actual threats. You do not encounter members of the Bloods, Crips, or other small time gang bangers without pissing somebody off.

I vividly remember being driven to a sentencing hearing in a shooting case by armed detectives from my office. They encouraged me to wear a bulletproof vest, and armed sharp-shooters were positioned on the roof for my protection.

After the sentencing, one of the sheriff's officers who transported the defendant from the jail to the courthouse told me I had nothing to worry about in the future from that defendant. He said that when they'd arrived at the courthouse, he pointed out the sharpshooters on the roof and said to the defendant, "This is all for you big shot, but in a few days, you will be hitting State's prison where you won't be a big shot anymore. You will be washing socks and sucking cocks." He said the defendant nearly soiled himself.

Back to the Monday Night Football afternoon. After clearing the metal detector checkpoint, I got on one of the elevators that would take me to my third-floor courtroom destination. While the building is only three stories, the ele-vators are extremely slow. The only other passenger on the elevator was a large African American male, and the way we were positioned in the elevator my back was to him. My experience told me that this guy, who was cut like a diamond, was either a professional athlete or had recently been released from prison. When he called me by name and asked, "You still prosecuting?" I became pretty sure he wasn't a professional athlete.

I then asked if I had prosecuted him, to which he

responded, "Oh yeah." Hoping to break the tension that was building, I asked him how I did. He said, "Pretty good, I got out of prison a few weeks ago after serving seventeen years."

The length of that sentence let me know that he was a violent offender, likely extremely dangerous. Having prosecuted thousands of cases, you not only forget defendant's names, but also the facts of most cases. My heart was racing as I asked him his name. When he told me it was "Deckie Davis," I could feel my balls in my throat. I clearly remembered the case, not only because "Deckie" is not a common first name, but because of the savagery of the attack on the victim.

Deckie was involved in a relationship with a woman who worked as a cashier at one of the Atlantic City casino buffets. After she broke it off, Deckie started harassing her, which culminated in him showing up while she was working one afternoon and stabbing her repeatedly. Luckily, an off-duty New York City police officer, in the middle of dining on crab legs and prime rib, was able to subdue Deckie and save her life.

At the time, the case had some local newsworthiness, probably more because of where, and not necessarily what, occurred. I recall my boss, the county prosecutor, asking me what charges I presented to the grand jury that indicted the case. When I told him one of the charges was attempted murder, he—who never let emotion be a part of his personality—told me I would never get a conviction on that count because it is so hard to prove. I told him the victim was stabbed seven times and he told me "so what," unimpressed with the proofs. I told him I had additional evidence that would sustain the charge, and when he pessimistically asked what it was,

I told him that in addition to Deckie stabbing the victim, he smashed her head with a cash register as she lay bleeding on the floor saying, "Die you fucking bitch!" To which the county prosecutor responded, "I guess you'll be okay with that evidence."

A lay person might find the prosecutor's inquiry shocking. However, most lawyers who spend years prosecuting criminal cases become desensitized to violence. You even reach a point where you can sit at your desk enjoying lunch while reviewing gruesome crime scene and autopsy photos. I guess after a while a person can get used to waterboarding too.

At the time of my elevator encounter with Deckie, I was in good physical shape. I was hitting the gym three times a week with some of my New Jersey state trooper buddies and bench pressing three hundred pounds. You should not be overly impressed by that, because I am short and squatty, which gives me a distinct advantage with bench presses; my arms do not need to travel as far as those of a taller person. It certainly did not give me any advantage over Deckie, who stands about six feet four inches tall.

My mind was racing. It swung between, "maybe I can get in one good blow to Deckie's groin before he chokes me out," and "at least if I'm killed in the line of duty on this elevator, my wife will get triple indemnity on my pension insurance." The elevator finally reached the third floor. A frightening journey ended with Deckie smiling at me, saying, "It was the bitch's fault." We parted ways and I praised God. I can't remember if the Bills won that night.

THE FACILITIES; A WALK-THROUGH

OF THE FOUR DIFFERENT PROSECUTOR'S office buildings I worked in, one of the facilities stands out as not just bad, but downright hazardous. For my first fifteen years, the office existed in a group of trailers that were a deemed a "temporary facility." It was a disaster. They had no windows, so staff constantly breathed putrid, recycled air. When it rained, the trailers leaked, and consequently black mold spread throughout. The restroom facilities were so bad that, in the final months before the trailers were condemned, portable toilets were placed in the parking lot for staff use.

As you might imagine, many staff members became seriously ill from having to work in these trailers. A considerable number, including those who were non-smokers, developed severe respiratory problems. There was a statistically high number of miscarriages given the population of the office, and several coworkers died from diverse types of cancer. A detective who was ordered to crawl underneath the trailers to run computer cables developed meningitis and was hospitalized.

A group of assistant prosecutors consulted an attorney about the working conditions and their illnesses. Unfortunately, because their illnesses were work-related, the only means of redress was Workers' Compensation. I do not know if they succeeded with their claims. Many of these coworkers moved on to other jobs as the laborious task of establishing their claims crawled through the Workers' Compensation process.

While OSHA came more than once to test air quality, the county government continued to assure us the numbers were acceptable. Many staff members suffered from headaches and symptoms conducive with chronic fatigue syndrome. This seriously contradicted what we were being told about the office air quality.

Why would the county government, knowing these terrible problems existed, continue to subject us to working in this facility? The answer is: to save a ton of money. What was particularly galling is that while we suffered, the governing body was touting the fact the county had a multi-million-dollar surplus. The long-serving county executive took a "lean" financial approach to government spending.

The problem with the trailers finally became public. An initial article in the local newspaper approached our circumstances as though they were humorous. A more serious reporter decided to dig deeper, and a subsequent article revealed that the situation was no laughing matter.

Shortly after the second article was printed, the county

executive announced that he was not seeking another term. The office rumor was that it had something to do with inaccurate reporting of air quality numbers. Whatever it was, we relocated within weeks to another temporary facility. The trailers were condemned, demolished, and the rubble was hauled away to an undisclosed dumpsite. Hopefully the same place where nuclear waste is disposed of.

The courthouse provided little refuge to the assistant prosecutors not forced to spend their entire workday in the trailers. It was a historically preserved structure that, while quaint, was also toxic.

Black mold again was the culprit that led the county to build a new courthouse. A sheriff's officer who was assigned to one of the courtrooms began suffering persistent respiratory problems. A spot was found on her lung, and she was diagnosed as having Stage 4 lung cancer. After seeking a second opinion from a specialist at the Center for Disease Control in Atlanta, it was determined that it was not to be cancer at all, but black mold. She eventually recovered.

The new courthouse and prosecutor's office were built adjoining one another, and were beautiful structures when finished. While the first few weeks in each building was eventful, the fact that the complex sits on a Lenape Indian burial ground was a bit foreboding.

The county government was anxious to get us into the new building so they could save a few hundred thousand dollars on the temporary space being rented. They realized too late that the HVAC system should have been running for a couple of weeks before the new structures became occupied.

The humidity left parts of the buildings dripping wet. Mold fostered in the evidence room, which had to be cleaned by workers in hazmat suits. Toilets exploded and pipes burst.

These problems could have resulted from construction or planning flaws. Many of us thought, however, that the Lenape Indians weren't so happy that these structures were built on their sacred ground.

The prosecutor's office victim/witness coordinator was a terrific person with a sense of gallows humor that helped get many staff members through difficult personal and professional times. She often joked with me about our years spent in the trailers and old courthouse saying, "You grew up down the road from the Love Canal, spent four years on an asbestos-filled Navy destroyer, and fifteen years in the trailers and old courthouse. You are a dead man walking!" She may have been right.

JUDGES

NO TWO CRIMINAL JUDGES ARE alike, but they essentially fit into three categories. Some are more liberal and lenient, others are state-oriented (i.e., do not tolerate criminal behavior at all), and a third group covet the power that comes with the position, but would rather be anywhere else. Trying cases with the first two is easy because, as a prosecutor, you can anticipate the judge's legal and evidentiary rulings and adjust your proofs accordingly. The last group is frustrating because of their unpredictable rulings.

If a judge is simply incompetent, but not arrogant, a prosecutor can still navigate the judge's shortcomings. However, when combined, arrogance and incompetence are an almost insurmountable hurdle for a prosecutor to overcome. The reason is that, despite any ineptitude, jurors will always perceive a judge as omniscient, abundantly fair, and emblematic of "truth, justice and the American way." No matter how much that judge hoses a prosecutor with abysmal rulings, the prosecutor must grin and bear it, because if the jury does not like the messenger, they are almost certain to reject the message.

When I found myself in a trial with a difficult judge, I tried to rely on sage advice my dad—who never attended law school, college, or even high school—gave me. "Son, if you have to eat shit, don't nibble." This is easier said than done, but as you will see, I always tried following that good advice.

One morning, as I was wrapping up a three-week trial, I told my wife to stay by the phone because she might need to post bail. When she asked me what I was talking about, I told her that I was quite likely to be held in contempt of court that day. This trial had been particularly heated, and I was at my wits' end. The three lawyers in the case were doing everything possible to distract from the facts, and they were being assisted by a judge who fit into a few of the categories previously described.

Judges are immensely powerful people in a courtroom, and their rulings on legal and evidentiary issues can seriously impact the outcome of a case. The most powerful tool—excluding knowledge and experience—that a judge can use to control what goes on in the courtroom is charging an attorney with contempt of court. The charge can be triggered by several behaviors, including habitual tardiness, failure to comply with a judge's order, or just outright disrespect for the judge. Usually, a judge does not need to charge contempt, because most attorneys are smart enough not to push a judge to the point where they could face fines, incarceration, and reprimand.

Back to that morning's trial. The case involved three

defendants who each unloaded their nine-millimeter hand-guns on a notoriously bad local guy. Despite their best efforts in firing some thirty rounds point blank at the victim, the shooters hit him only six times, and he survived. It wasn't the first or the last time this victim had been shot. To this day, I am sure that he has more lead in him than a pencil.

The shooting occurred in front of a bar/restaurant on a busy thoroughfare. In fact, several witnesses who testified at trial were driving by at the time of the shooting, and their vehicles were hit by ricochets. The restaurant was not only famous for its food, but also for the number of shootings that occurred there. I remember one fatal shooting where the establishment's security video showed patrons casually step-ping over a victim who lay dying at the front entrance. My colleagues and I would joke that you do not dine there unless you wanted to get lead poisoning.

Anyway, for three weeks, the three defense attorneys had their way with the state's witnesses because this disinterested judge (who truly was one of the most gracious gentlemen you could meet outside of a courtroom) believed that the Rules of Evidence and Procedure should not get in the way of "com-pleteness of the record." While it is important to show defer-ence to the judge for the reason I discussed earlier, at times a jury (particularly if they are with you) do not want to see you as some weak, ass-kissing sycophant either.

As we continued the trial that morning, and defense counsel repeatedly asked questions that were irrelevant and immaterial, I objected seven straight times on the grounds that the questions were just that. Each time, the judge would respond to my objection simply with, "Overruled." The first six times, I sat down without any comment. The seventh time, I may have responded, "Withdrawn, I know which way it's going." The judge suddenly became interested in the trial, asking the sheriff's officer to remove the jury, and ordering me to chambers before storming off the bench.

Realizing that the judge was pissed, I asked the stenographer to join us, so I would at least have a record of our discussion from which to appeal any contempt finding. By the time she and I reached chambers, the judge was fuming. "That's it, Mister, if you don't go out there and apologize to me in front of the jury you will be held in contempt," he raged.

I calmly asked, "Judge what's the problem?"

"You know what you said out there," he said.

"What do you think I said?"

"You said, 'I know which way it's going,'" he replied.

"No, no," I said, "I believe my exact words were, 'withdrawn, I know which way he's going.' Knowing that I had touched upon that subject on my direct, I withdrew my seventh objection since it was proper cross-examination by defense counsel." The judge said that was "bullshit," and asked the stenographer to read back my objection. She said since both the judge and I were talking at the same time, she was not able to record what was said with specificity.

This whole back-and-forth took about thirty minutes, and by the time we returned, the courtroom was packed with lawyers and staff anxious to see if the prosecutor was going to be locked up or at least fined. The jury had a clear picture of what was going on, and when the judge said, "The prosecutor has something to say to me," they gave me a nearly unanimous sympathetic glance. I stood and said, "Judge, I am sorry that you misunderstood me." After another thirty minutes of fast talking in chambers—and a bit of luck, because the judge was a decent man—I was not held in contempt. I fared much better than the three shooters, who were sentenced to some serious time after being found guilty on all charges.

The most exasperating moments of a prosecutor's career are during trials with a judge who is more arrogant than competent. I am sure every criminal courthouse has at least one. This is the type of judge who needs to know everything that's going to happen during the trial in advance of it happening, doesn't trust the prosecutor or defense counsel when they offer sound legal advice because the judge thinks either or both is trying to screw him, and once the trial starts, wants it over yesterday.

One of my colleagues was so devastated by a judge's ruling that she never wanted to try a case again. The defendant in her case shot his victim in the back of the head at close range, and the shooting was caught on videotape. Even after the defense attorney admitted in opening statements that his client shot the victim, the judge denied the prosecutor's motion to allow the jury to consider aggravated manslaughter or manslaughter, which are the lesser included offenses of murder. If there is a rational basis in the evidence to instruct the jury on lesser included offenses, the jury is permitted and instructed to consider these lesser included charges in reaching a just verdict. When the judge refused to so instruct them—most likely assuming that no rational jury would convict on any charge

other than murder—the jury concluded that it was not a murder, and having no option to convict the defendant of manslaughter, found him not guilty.

There is some shit that is just too hard to swallow.

I know I worked backwards in addressing the several
types of judges, but there is little to be said about the good
ones. Within the group who possessed conservative or liberal
natures, existed a subset who were fair, patient, and dedicated
to the rule of law. They would let each side present its case
within the Rules of Evidence and Procedure, awarded creativity, seldom if ever tried to embarrass any of the participants,
and left their egos at the door in administering justice.

These types of judges made trying cases a pleasure. In
Atlantic County, prosecutors and defense counsel were lucky
to have more than one of them. And one judge happened
to be the best in the State of New Jersey, never having been
reversed on appeal. Not only was he well-versed in both substantive and procedural law, but he also had a great, albeit wry,
sense of humor, and the patience of Job.

One of my colleagues had secured a conviction in a brutal and disgusting sexual assault case tried by this judge. The
defendant had slashed his victim's face with a knife from her
ear to the corner of her mouth, and then forced her to perform oral sex on him.

When the defendant was being sentenced, I happened to
be in the courtroom on other matters. Before being sentenced,
every convicted defendant has a right of allocution—the right
to speak on their own behalf. This defendant stayed true to his
vile nature, in that he engaged in a fifteen-minute profane and

anti-Semitic tirade against the judge, who listened patiently before imposing an enhanced sentence that sent the defendant away for the rest of his life. Later, when we were talking in his chambers, I told the judge—whom I had been assigned to for seven years—that I had never seen him more patient than he had been in that sentencing. He looked at me with his patented grin and said, "Why be upset? Numbers speak louder than words." I salute those exceptional judges—some of whom have passed—for their dedication and thank them for all they taught me.

A JUDGE WITH CHARACTER, WHO WAS A CHARACTER

TWO OF THE MOST FUN years during my career as a prosecutor were spent in the courtroom of a judge who not only had character but was a character. There were so many interesting and funny moments spent with him that picking out the best is difficult. The first thing to know about him is that if he wasn't busting your balls, then he really did not like you. The second was that his physical stature and demeanor were like the cartoon character Yosemite Sam. He was short, stout, and unafraid to vent anytime and anywhere.

This judge's wit was razor sharp and his sense of humor was robust. He had a good heart, which led him to ignore the law quite often in the interest of doing what was right. I know he did not appreciate attorneys who were arrogant or sleazy, and he particularly despised anyone who committed crimes against old people or animals. That was probably because of what he cherished most in life: his elderly parents and his dog. He'd been an assistant prosecutor for several years before being appointed to the bench.

What he lacked in height he made up for with a Napoleonic complex. To counter it, the sheriff's officer assigned to his court room would occasionally wind down the swivel chair behind the judge's bench so when the judge came in and took his seat, all that was visible over the bench was the top of his head. He always took this prank in stride, which was a testament to his profound sense of humor. His greatest weakness was that he was germophobic, which made him squeamish and vulnerable to pranking. I remember a case I tried with him that revealed this vulnerability.

The case involved what was a common scenario for Atlantic City: two hookers (prostitutes) and a casino patron. As the patron was leaving the casino with his wife, he was jostled by one hooker while the other pickpocketed him for a couple thousand dollars. The two hookers then split up the money, concealing it in their vaginas in the event they were apprehended by police. They were apprehended, police conducted a legal body cavity search of their persons, and the patron's money was recovered.

I was feeling mischievous on the morning of closing arguments and decided to stop by the judge's chambers with defense counsel for a little fun. Catching him off guard, I asked the judge in a serious tone if I could tell the jurors that it was the prosecution's position that the defendants had "snatched" the patron's money. "No, no, no," he replied, telling me that an appellate court would not look kindly on such a comment. I then asked him in a more serious tone if I could say they placed the money in their cash "boxes." I knew I had him because he was now getting angry and told me, "Absolutely not, and don't be putting that filthy money anywhere near my bench." I assured him I would not, and that I'd avoid handling it during the trial by picking up the money up in my teeth. Upon hearing this, he made a beeline for his private restroom. When he emerged, and knowing he was had, he enjoyed a good laugh with us.

The judge was admired for keeping things light even in the most serious trials. On one such occasion, he gruffly summoned defense counsel and me to sidebar at a very emotional time in a homicide case. I recall some of the jurors were wiping tears from their eyes, and we both had no clue as to what the judge wanted from us. When we got to sidebar he said, "Have you boys ever seen that old baseball movie, where it's the bottom of the ninth, the bases are loaded, the team at bat trails by one run, there are two outs, the count is three balls, two strikes, the catcher calls timeout, walks out to the mound to talk with the pitcher and while everyone in the stadium thinks they are talking about the next pitch, they are actually talking about where they are going fishing after the game? Isn't this one of those moments?" He then told us to get back to work, and if either one of us laughed about what he just said, he would lock us both up for contempt of court.

It was a blessing that he retired before the advent of video courtrooms. The judge wore his emotions on his sleeve, and whenever a witness was testifying falsely, he would start inspecting his fingernails in a manner suggesting that witness had nothing to contribute. It did not matter whether the witness was testifying for the defense or the prosecution. Occasionally, when the witness got completely out of control in testifying falsely, the judge would give the internationally recognized sign for "jerkoff."

He was not just entertaining during trials; he brought fun to everyday court proceedings too. Mondays in court were usually dedicated to calling a long arraignment/status conference list. Trials normally were held between Tuesdays and Thursdays, and Fridays were reserved for sentencings and pre-trial motions. When he would call the list on Monday, he would calmly announce to the courtroom full of attorneys and defendants that anyone arriving late would be "locked up, including attorneys." This did not serve to warn those who came late, but it deterred those present from arriving late in the future. And he often made good on that threat. Although he was more tolerant of tardiness from attorneys, I do remember one time he had an attorney who was habitually late put in a holding cell for the rest of the day.

Fridays were really the days for the judge to shine. As previously stated, the judge had a soft spot for old people. Anytime a defendant's elderly parent spoke on the defendant's behalf at sentencing, the judge appeared moved and would shave some time off the prosecutor's sentencing recommendation. Conversely, he hated when defendants would bring their children to sentencing. The defendant would plead with him not to impose a prison sentence because no one else could care for the children. The judge had a good sense of who was using children as a prop, and on those occasions, he would slide his glasses to the end of his nose, leer at them, and ask, "What, do you think you are some sort of a role model?"

I once witnessed him sentence a defendant who one of my colleagues prosecuted for selling a large quantity of heroin. In addition to a twenty-year sentence, the judge imposed mandatory fines totaling several thousand dollars. The defendant was muttering as he was being led from the court room in shackles, and the judge told the sheriff's officers to "bring him back here." The judge then asked, "Do you have a problem?" The defendant replied, "Yeah, I have a problem." The judge asked, "What's your problem?" To which the defendant responded, "How am I gonna pay them fines?" The judge was so impressed (and humored) by the defendant being more concerned about the fines getting paid than he was about the length of the sentence, that he reduced it by two years. I remember thinking, now there is a guy who takes "paying his debt to society" seriously.

The judge loved to eat and drink. It may be more accurate to say that he loved to eat and lived to drink. He particularly enjoyed eating lobster, and bourbon was a food group to him.

For many years, and to this day, my family and I vacation in Maine every Summer. Each year I was assigned to his courtroom, and for several years afterward, he would give me money to bring him back a cooler full of live Maine lobsters. I never minded doing this because we became good friends. Though bringing him the lobsters didn't come without stress.

I would never hear the end of it if one or more of his lobsters did not survive the trip. To avoid his wrath, I would drop my wife and kids off at home, and before unloading the car,

I would head right to the judge's house with the lobsters. He was always grateful to receive them and would insist that I stay for a drink. I fondly remember the very first time I brought him lobsters. He asked me what I would like to drink, and when I told him I would like a beer he replied, "Only barbarians drink beer after 9 o'clock."

He then proceeded to pour me a milk glass full of bourbon. Not being a bourbon drinker at the time, I started rummaging through his refrigerator looking for a can of Coke to mix with and dilute the bourbon. He asked me what I was doing, and when I told him, he said in his snarly voice, "You mix anything with that good bourbon, and I'll kill you." We spent the next hour or so chatting because that's how long it took for me to choke down the bourbon. Before I could head for the door, he poured me another glassful. It took another hour to finish that one, and since it was now around midnight, I told him that I absolutely needed to head home. Always looking out for me, he said, "You better be careful driving. You had an awful lot to drink tonight."

I felt honored when asked to speak at the judge's retirement party. While most of the other speakers roasted him, I chose to remember him as always striving to do what was just and fair, no matter the consequences. He was often criticized, and several of his decisions were reversed by appellate courts for not following the law. These appellate decisions never dissuaded his personal pursuit of justice and fairness.

He retired, moved south, and returned once a year to have lunch with fellow judges who were still working. In the last years of his life, his memory began to slip precipitously, and his last visit was memorable. The prosecutor's office abuts the new courthouse, and I am sure the judge thought he was entering the courthouse when he could not get through a secured door. One of the secretaries, who did not know him, was outside having a cigarette as he tried to enter through the door. He was frustrated when he could not get in and said to the secretary, "Let me in. What do I have to do, shoot you to get in here?" This might not have been so dramatic had the office staff not just completed Active Shooter Training. Luckily, a detective who knew the judge—and just as importantly, who the judge recognized—was the first to respond to the situation, and simply escorted the judge to the Courthouse.

The judge ended up living the last years of his life in a skilled nursing facility's memory unit. His passing marked the end of the life of a judge with character, who was a character.

THE HUNT

COUNTY DETECTIVES ARE INVALUABLE PERSONNEL in any prosecutor's office. They are important because they act as intermediaries between the prosecutors and the municipal police officers, who often feel that once they have made the arrest and handed over an "airtight" (in their minds) case, the job is over. In most cases, there is additional work to be done, and the responsibility for bringing the case to conclusion lies with the detectives. Among other duties, they run down missing case reports, request any additional forensic testing of evidence, conduct additional witness interviews, and track down witnesses to ensure their presence at trial.

A lay person might be surprised by how often a prosecutor needs to hunt down reluctant witnesses. Logic seems to dictate that a victim or witness would be eager to see justice served. However, there are good reasons that victims and witnesses might be reluctant to come forward, one of them being a fear of retaliation from the criminal or his associates. "Snitches get stitches" was the mantra in the hood for most of my career. There are bad reasons to avoid taking the stand too. On more than one occasion, I encountered people who wanted to get retribution for themselves; street justice as it were.

You'd think it would be a burden, but locating and trying to convince reluctant witnesses to appear at trial was the most fun part of the job. It was like a game of hide and seek for adults. The next three stories are dedicated to some of these hunts and the detectives who led them.

County Detective Sergeant Randy Washington was an older African American gentleman who lived most of his life in Atlantic City. He was active in the community, including being a coach for youth sports. Consequently, Randy knew many if not most Atlantic City residents and had a tremendous rapport with them. He also had a keen sense of humor, a tremendous understanding of human behavior, and a powerful sense of what was just.

Whenever a prosecutor exhausted all efforts to locate a missing witness, it was time to put Sergeant Washington on it. Randy was proud of his ability to find them. He boasted about a time the chief of county detectives ordered him to find a missing witness in an important homicide case within three days—or not bother coming back to the job. Randy found the witness within thirty minutes and took the next three days off.

All county detectives are required to carry a handgun, and Randy was no exception. He would be the first person to tell you that he was not a good shot. Twice a year, when it came time to requalify, you could tell that he was nervous because he smoked more Lucky Strikes than usual. In fact, Randy often joked that the way he would get difficult witnesses to honor a trial subpoena was to tell them not to run. He would say, "If you run, I might have to shoot you, and I'm not a very good shot. I'll try and hit you in the ass, but I might hit you in the head."

Another memory I have of Randy is that on occasion, when I was in trial with a defendant and jurors who were people of color, Randy would stop by. Although he had no part in the case, he would sit down next to me, put his arm on my shoulder, and whisper absolute nonsense in my ear. The first time he did this he told me that he just wanted me to have a "level playing field."

Randy had remarkable stories. Before he became involved in law enforcement, his primary job was as a bouncer in a pre-casino nightclub in Atlantic City. The nightclub drew top notch entertainers, and he told me about one night when a blind performer of note was so intoxicated that he went on stage to perform with his back to the audience. Randy had to turn him around.

We became good friends, and both of us shared a passion for Polish sausage (kielbasa). Every time I returned to my native North Tonawanda, New York, I would bring him a couple pounds. It was sad to see him leave for his well-earned retirement, and even sadder when he passed a few years later.

I maintain a top ten list in my head of people I would want by my side if I found myself walking down a dark alley fraught with danger. One of those persons would be retired Detective Lieutenant Janet LaRocca, who was the first woman assigned to the Prosecutor's Office Major Crime Squad (MCS). The MCS investigates all homicides occurring in the county.

Janet was not only particularly good at hunting witnesses down, but she also excelled at getting the truth from witnesses once she found them. She is small in stature, sweet as pie, and tough as nails, a combination which served her well and made her extremely good at what she did.

My fondest memory of working with Janet came during a visit she and I made to one of South Jersey's state prisons to speak with a crucial witness in a homicide case she had investigated. My assigned detective and I had been there weeks before to speak with this same witness, who shut down and told us that "Detective Janet" had assured him that he would never have to testify.

When we got back to the office, Janet asked me how the trial prep went, and I told her that the witness was stonewalling us. She was livid and asked my detective to arrange a second prison visit.

She and I met with this witness, and she did not waste any time lighting him up. He immediately admitted that she had never told him he would not have to testify, but Janet did not stop there. She told him not to play that "fear of retaliation bullshit" with her as it was urban legend, and the fact that he presently found himself serving a sentence was proof positive he was not shy in confronting dangerous situations. The interview went well, and I recall that he did well in testifying truthfully at trial.

That afternoon on our drive back from the prison, I remember telling Janet that she had used words I had never heard in four years as a Navy fleet sailor. She got a kick out of that, and during the remainder of the hour or so drive back to the office we discussed church music. Back then we both sang in our respective church choirs.

It is crucial for a trial prosecutor to work with detectives who are tough, experienced, and know when to be kind-yet-firm with victims to help take the bad guys who victimized them off the streets. Most of the newly hired detectives in the office pass through the trial section. During my twenty-five years as a prosecutor, I was assigned at least twelve different detectives, and none of them considered trial work to be a punishment or beneath their investigative skills.

A good detective can make or break a trial prosecutor. The detective is your right hand, not only helping you physically prepare a case for trial but also acting as your sounding board. A detective who gives brutally honest critiques of your performance as the trial progresses is an invaluable asset. If you try a lot of cases, you spend a lot of time with your detective, and a good rapport improves the entire process.

I was assigned many outstanding detectives, but one that stood out was Detective Lieutenant Les Folks. He had been assigned to MCS for many years, and when for some reason there was an office reorganization, Les was sent to trial. He could have been bitter, since trial work would not be as challenging as his many years in MCS, but he was not. Normally, a prosecutor cannot ask for a better trial detective than a former street cop; their years spent on the street create good instincts. In Lieutenant Folks I did even better. He had one year of law school before deciding that a career in law enforcement was what he really wanted to do, and he was an excellent detective.

I read something recently that reminded me of Les. "There are only three choices you can make in life: give up, give in, or give it all you got." Les always gave his all, and like me, he enjoyed the hunt. We spent many hours together pursuing and preparing witnesses for trial. He always had my back, and to this day, I would walk through a wall of fire for him.

One of the many cases Les and I tried involved a serial rapist, and it was one of the most memorable of my career. The victim was a single mom with three children, living in a multi-story rooming house in Atlantic City. Each floor had a common bathroom with a bathtub/shower shared by others who lived on that floor. I remember being impressed the first time I met her at her residence. She was managing to raise her three well-kempt children in a one-room dwelling, and all of them were studiously doing their homework on the afternoon I was there.

The day she was sexually assaulted had been a frigid winter evening. She was playing outside of the building with her young daughter when both had to use the bathroom. The daughter said, "I'll race you, Mom!" For better or worse, the victim got to the bathroom first. Unbeknownst to her, the defendant was hiding behind the shower curtain in the bathtub. When she sat down on the toilet, the defendant viciously attacked her. He shoved a scarf she was wearing in her mouth to silence her screams, and he sexually penetrated her with his fingers and penis. He then sodomized her with a quart beer bottle.

She passed out, and when she awoke the defendant was gone, and she was lying on the floor bleeding from her rectum and vagina. The victim was able to give the police a fully accurate description of the defendant, and the quart beer bottle was recovered at the scene. As it turns out, the defendant worked as an aide at a nearby nursing home. To this day, I shudder to think what this serial rapist may have done to elderly, incapacitated persons there.

The police were able to lift a thumbprint from the bottle, which matched that of the defendant. In my twenty-five years of prosecuting thousands of cases, it was the only case I ever had with a latent fingerprint that was "usable" at trial (more later on fingerprint evidence and the myth that one will always be found).

Rape victims are much different than victims of any other crimes. As in this case, they have been violated and defiled, usually experiencing a paralytic fear during the rape that leaves them feeling responsible for what occurred. Establishing a rapport with the victim is critical to a successful prosecution, and it is essential that a victim implicitly trusts your honest attempt to restore even a small part of their stolen dignity.

Les and I kept in contact with this victim over the many months leading up to trial and thought we had convinced her that she and her children would be safe from the defendant, who we told her would rightfully spend the rest of his life in prison if convicted. It is important to always say "if" to maintain a victim's trust, because there are no guarantees with a jury.

But like juries, often there are no guarantees with victims

and witnesses, and even though Les and I were convinced that she would appear at trial, she disappeared the day before she was scheduled to testify. As soon as Les heard she was missing, he grabbed his coat and said, "I'll find her."

As dawn of the next day broke, and after hours of preparing for the day's trial testimony, I still hadn't heard anything from Les. By the time I arrived at the courthouse and got myself situated, I started to feel sick to my stomach; Les was nowhere to be found, and the victim was my next witness.

When the sheriff's officers brought the defendant in and unshackled him, he had this smug look on his face, as if he knew she wasn't going to appear and that the charges against him would then be dismissed. My gut wrenched knowing that this bastard might get away with this vile crime because he so terrified the victim while committing it.

When the judge said, "Prosecutor, call your next witness," I was prepared to start groveling for a continuance of the case to give us additional time to find the victim. At that moment, as if scripted by a screenwriter, the courtroom door flew open and in came the witness escorted by a very tired and disheveled Les. I later came to find that Les had spent all night attempting to locate her by talking with anyone and everyone who knew her, and surveilling every place she might be. Eventually, he'd been able to calm her fears and convince her that testifying was the only way she could truly put this horror behind her.

The defense's cross-examination was brutal and humiliating; she was accused of consenting to the sex. She held up remarkably well on the witness stand. Les and I kept our promise that she and her children would be safe "if" the defendant were convicted. He was convicted and sentenced to life in prison because of two prior sexual assault convictions he'd had in New York, which were eerily similar, but were plea bargained because of his prior victims' fear of testifying. He died in prison some years later. Les' thirty-four years of dedicated service were recognized by a promotion, and he retired as captain of Homicide.

The hunt was a significant part of prosecuting cases. Without crucial witness testimony there would be no trial. And without the dedication and determination of these detectives, who ensured a witness's presence at trail, there would be no justice for victims or their survivors.

PUBLIC DEFENDER, A THANKLESS JOB

ONCE CRIMINAL DEFENDANTS ARE CHARGED, there is an initial appearance before a judge. The first question the judge asks is whether the defendant is represented by an attorney. Customarily, defendants respond that they are not, and the judge asks whether they intend to hire their own attorney. Most defendants then tell the judge that they have no money to hire an attorney, and the judge tells them to apply for the services of a public defender. Nine of ten first-time defendants then respond, "I don't want no public defender. I want a real lawyer."

Every time I heard a defendant say this, I would think of Lorraine Stanley, my best friend from law school, and a very good friend to this day. Lorraine retired several years ago after a career with a public defender's office in a northern New Jersey County. She was born and raised in Jersey City as one of five children in an Irish Catholic family. Lorraine is an extremely bright, tough, impassioned, and talented attorney.

If I ever find myself criminally charged, I want Lorraine representing me.

Before I get too far ahead of myself, let me describe how Lorraine and I met. Another law school friend and I were sitting around the cafeteria one month into our first year. As we discussed the previous day's NFL games, we broached the topic of forming a study group. It is almost impossible to get through law school without one, given the amount of material covered in any semester. Knowing that we were weeks behind our classmates who were already in study groups, we decided to form one soon, then went back to talking football.

As though God himself sent her, we noticed Lorraine sitting down next to us. She was in tears, and we asked what was wrong and if we could help. Lorraine explained to us that she was invited to join a study group by some of our more "popular" classmates, and when she went to where they told her they were meeting, none of them was there. It was their way of telling Lorraine they felt she did not belong in law school.

Your first inclination might be that the students who did that cruel thing to Lorraine were total assholes. And you would be right. Law schools are strange places. Anyone gaining admission usually finished near the top of their undergraduate class and is surrounded by classmates who are similarly situated. Being average is hard for some people to accept, particularly if they are as arrogant as the group Lorraine encountered.

Without missing a beat, my friend and I asked Lorraine if she wanted to join our study group. She asked when we met, and we told her, "Why not right now?" It was the beginning of a beautiful friendship. We worked hard and played hard, usually finding the time for a couple of beers every day. In some courses we did quite well, and in most we accepted the fact that we were average. We surprised many of our classmates by graduating.

Jersey City, where Lorraine grew up, is a hardworking, ethnically diverse city just across the river from New York. Over the years it has become gentrified, but it was a neighborhood community when Lorraine was raised there. She had the benefit of a solid Catholic school education and a loving family, a family that accepted me as one of its members when we became law school friends. Like her other siblings, Lorraine is a good athlete, which fueled her fiercely competitive nature.

Lorraine's mom, a college professor, instilled in her a profound sense of social justice, and her dad was truly one of the finest gentlemen I have ever met. Lorraine worked as a social worker before entering law school and has always been a champion for society's downtrodden. She has a great heart, is a loyal friend, tells it like it is (sometimes in colorful language), and never surrenders. All these qualities made Lorraine a great asset to the public defender's office, and defendants were fortunate to have her as their attorney.

I always thought of Lorraine when defendants would comment on wanting a "real lawyer," because I've seen the dedication she and the public defenders I worked with have. People are often heard to ask how anyone could work as a public defender representing guilty people. Newsflash! Not all persons charged are guilty of the crimes they are accused of.

Additionally, prosecutors often over-indict cases. This is not to say that they charge crimes for which there is no evidence, but sometimes they charge crimes that marginally fall within a particular criminal statute. These occasions require public defenders to carefully review the evidence, explain to the defendant which crimes the prosecution can prove, and then convince the prosecutor of what might be a fair disposition of the charges.

Public defenders also ensure, from arrest to acquittal or conviction, that a defendant's constitutional rights are not violated. They are duty-bound to try a case if that is what their client elects to do. A defendant's guilt or innocence isn't important—they are ethically bound to zealously represent all clients.

Most courtrooms in New Jersey are staffed with two prosecutors, each matched with a public defender. Only a small percentage of cases eventually go to trial because most cases end in a guilty plea, not to mention that the sheer volume of cases makes it impossible to try them all. Many judges are overly conscious of how many cases they dispose of each month. A public defender who I was very fond of once told me, "We are all just whores for the list pimp."

In order to move cases justly and expeditiously, it is important that the prosecutor and public defender have a good rapport. This requires trust between a prosecutor and public defender. I can honestly say I was never low-balled by a public defender. The same did not hold true for all private counsel, some of whom I never saw again.

No matter how much judges think they control a

courtroom, without a competent and capable public defender, things can slow to a complete halt. It isn't unusual for a public defender to spend seven hours in a holding cell talking to incarcerated defendants on a "jail day." I know how many times I was "motherfucked" in getting reluctant witnesses to appear, and that multiplied by ten is what a public defender who is not mentally tough faces in a single week. It takes a special type of person with grit and determination to do the work effectively.

I dedicate this chapter to my friend Lorraine, and all her sister and brother public defenders. I will always respect their selfless dedication to pursuing just results for their clients in what is often a thankless job.

JURORS

IF I LEARNED ANYTHING DURING my twenty-five years of prosecuting criminal cases, it was that jury selection was the single most important part of the process. Pick the wrong jury, and you usually get an unfavorable result. I should modify that last statement to say, "pick the wrong juror," because a single juror has the capacity to prevent a just result. Any way you slice it, jury selection is a crapshoot. Both sides need to determine whether among the twelve people selected, and with the limited number of questions asked by the judge during their selection, they picked the right ones.

Residing in the county gave you an advantage in jury selection because you were familiar with a community's values. One particular town was my favorite to select from because, in my experience, they would convict their own mother if she were the defendant. Conversely, I always shied away from selecting any prospective juror from another town possessing equally conservative values because those jurors always hung the jury, even in cases where the evidence supporting conviction was strong. I assumed that there was something different in the drinking water in that community.

Whether the defendant was convicted or not, it was my experience that the jury usually reached the right conclusion based upon the evidence and everything else that went on in the courtroom during the trial. Jurors are not only influenced by the evidence, but also by the behavior of all the participants.

There were occasional incidents with juries that stood out. I recall one such incident during a homicide trial. The case involved a gay couple with a tumultuous and violent history. Police went to their residence many times responding to allegations of domestic abuse. On any given day, it could be the victim or defendant who was the aggressor. The last one occurred when the defendant stabbed his partner in the chest, killing him. The victim had AIDS and was wearing a down jacket at the time of the stabbing. After reading an article about airborne pathogens, I took special precautions in handling the victim's bloodied clothing both before and during the trial, wearing surgical gloves and avoiding direct skin contact with it.

Anyway, I wanted to be especially cautious in handling the evidence during trial because the foreperson of the jury looked to be eight months pregnant, and she was sitting in the front row of the jury box. When the time came to identify the victim's jacket, I gloved up and carefully opened the evidence bag to remove it. Feathers started flying and floating everywhere. I was aghast, but we got through the testimony without too much chaos. During the entire testimony of the next witness, I noticed one of the jurors staring at a vent directly above him.

The judge took a morning recess, and while he, defense counsel, and I were chatting in chambers, the assigned sheriff's officer brought in a note from one of the jurors. The note was written by the juror who had been staring at the vent and said that he "had an idea of where the moths were coming from." We all immediately knew that he thought the feathers from the jacket were moths, and when I told the judge that the juror had been staring at the vent, he had the whole picture. The judge asked whether we had any suggestions as to how he might answer the juror's question. Both of us laughed, telling him we had none, and that's why judges get the big money.

When we went back after the recess, the judge told the sheriff's officer to bring the jury back to the courtroom. Without any prior collaboration, both defense counsel and I started swatting the air. All of us were laughing so hard that he had to stop the officer from bringing the jury back in. In fact, it took three attempts and about fifteen minutes before we composed ourselves enough to resume the trial.

A trial attorney should never assume that a jury is "getting it," and that stating a point two or three times is redundant. In fact, when trying a case, it is good practice to say the same thing repeatedly in different ways. The subtle way a prosecutor can do this is to have the witness tell the story through initial questioning, then have the witness tell it a second and third time by questioning the witness using photographs and diagrams that are part of the evidence in a case.

It is also necessary to explain the law and the indictment to the jury during summation, highlighting the important points. In this way, the jury can focus on what matters to the prosecution, ensuring it doesn't get lost in a two- or three-hour jury instruction from the judge at the trial's end. One such example of this happening was in a case tried by a colleague. The case involved a single count of possession of a weapon, to wit, a handgun. The defendant had the gun on his person and did not have a permit to carry it.

From start to finish, the trial lasted two hours—the facts of the case couldn't have been clearer. When the jury was still deliberating late into its second day, my colleague, defense counsel, and the judge were puzzled. The mystery was solved when the jury sent a note to the judge asking what "to wit" meant. When the judge informed them that the phrase was defined as "stating something more precisely," the jury went back into deliberations and had a guilty verdict in under five minutes.

As currently divided as this country is politically, I am grateful to be retired. Getting twelve people who are chosen randomly to agree on anything nowadays is seemingly impossible. It wasn't that easy ten years ago either. The old courthouse referred to in previous chapters was not spacious, and the jury deliberation rooms were within earshot of passageways adjoining judges' chambers. When deliberations got hot, the jurors could be heard shouting at one another.

I recall a case where jury deliberations were entering a third day after a four-day trial, and things were heating up. There was a shouting match going on between individual jurors, and periodically, some jurors could be heard slamming their hands on the table in the room to emphasize a point. The jury sent a note to the judge on day three of deliberations saying, "We are deadlocked. Things are getting heated in here, and there may be violence." As required, he asked defense counsel and me for suggestions on how to respond. I told him to send in twelve pairs of boxing gloves. He must have thought I was serious because he said, "Oh my, we can't do that. I must declare a mistrial." Defense counsel and I subsequently worked the case out by means of a guilty plea. Not a single punch was thrown.

Another thing learned from prosecuting cases over twenty-five years is how difficult it is to predict what a jury is thinking. I once tried a drug case which was neither the most substantial nor exciting case of my career. As I was giving my closing argument, half the jurors seemed riveted to my every word and were nodding their heads in agreement on the more significant points of my argument. To say the other half of the jury looked disinterested would be a gross understatement. Anyway, after two days of deliberations, the jury announced that it was "hopelessly" deadlocked, and the judge declared a mistrial. As I was walking to my car, the six "nodding" jurors approached me en masse. They very politely told me that they were the six jurors who voted for acquittal, and that they wanted to tell me why. Their logic was sound, and I felt incredibly good about the fact that they had taken their oath to reach a fair and just verdict seriously, despite the charges not being particularly significant.

I said previously that jury selection is a crapshoot;

sometimes you make your point, and other times you roll snake eyes. However, while the jury system is not perfect, it is better than most.

MEMORABLE WITNESSES

THERE ARE SOME WITNESSES I encountered in my career, who by their very nature and/or their responses to questions posed during the trial, are indelibly etched in my mind. In some instances, I was moved by the struggles people overcame after having been victimized, and in others, I was amused by their honest and hilarious answers alone. Occasionally, those responses came in cases tried by colleagues that I was merely observing.

Not all victims and witnesses are uncooperative, and occasionally, you get a witness that goes out of their way to assist you in preparing for trial. One such victim who comes to mind was a victim of an aggravated assault who lost sight in his left eye after being stabbed in the face. His only request was that we meet him at his job to do trial prep, so that he wouldn't miss any work. That was not a problem for my detective and I, since we were always willing to accommodate cooperative witnesses, especially in serious cases.

This fellow asked us to meet him on the Atlantic City

Boardwalk in front of one of the casinos. It was a wet and blustery March day, and the wind whipping off the ocean made it quite unpleasant. A few minutes after we arrived, we looked up and found our victim. He was washing windows six stories up on a scaffold, and when he saw us, gestured that he would be down shortly. The moment he was back on the street, we could smell the whiskey on his breath from several feet away.

He was a very decent guy who we came to learn was a Vietnam veteran. After we concluded our interview, and without mentioning the fact that he had obviously been drinking, I asked him how he could stand on a scaffold on a rainy and windy day, six stories up, washing windows with only one eye. He smiled and said, "In order to make real money you have to go above five stories."

I thought that no one could go higher than my window washer victim until I tried a homicide case involving iron workers, one a victim and the other a defendant. These two guys had been working together on a high-rise project in Atlantic City.

This workday was going as usual for them. They were stories above the street, balancing on a girder, and consuming large quantities of alcohol and illegal substances. Their consumption continued through lunch, and when the workday ended, they went to the defendant's house to continue the party, stopping first to purchase some cocaine.

Around midnight, the victim decided he was going to drive home, and the defendant, having a rational moment, told the victim he was too intoxicated to drive and should spend the night. The victim took exception to the defendant's suggestion, and a fist fight occurred in the defendant's driveway. Had it been a sanctioned bout, it may have been stopped early on because the victim absorbed quite a beating. Now too drunk, high, and injured to drive, the victim decided to stay.

The next morning was pay day, and the defendant was unable to wake the victim (because he was comatose), so he picked him up, placed him in the rear seat of his truck, and drove to the jobsite. When they arrived, the supervisor asked the defendant where the victim was. The defendant explained to the supervisor that the two had been partying the night before, and the victim was sleeping it off in the back of the truck. The supervisor then told the defendant that if the victim wasn't working within an hour, the victim would be docked a day's pay.

When the defendant and supervisor returned to the truck an hour later, the victim was dead. As unusual and interesting as these facts may seem, the most memorable part of the case for me was talking with the supervisor in preparation for trial. I was trying to produce a timeline as to when significant events occurred the evening before to determine the victim's time of death.

Most if not all forensic pathologists will tell you that what you see in movies and on television in terms of determining an exact time of death is a bunch of hooey. In my experience, the medical examiner— a pathologist—would ask you when the victim was last seen alive and what time they were found dead. They would then tell you the time of death was sometime between the two.

In this case, if I were able to calculate with reasonable certainty how much alcohol the victim consumed, I could come close to determining when the victim died because the body breaks down alcohol at a certain rate per hour. When a person dies, the body stops breaking down the alcohol and the level remains constant. As part of an autopsy, blood and other body fluids are gathered for toxicological testing, and a known alcohol level is established through the testing. Why was all of this so important to the case? I wanted to know if the victim was dead when the defendant put him in the back seat of the truck.

The defendant had admitted to detectives at the time of his arrest that he and the victim had consumed a pint of brandy, a twelve pack of beer, and smoked a joint during the workday. He also detailed how much they drank and how much cocaine they snorted prior to the fight. The missing link for me was how much they drank at lunch.

To that end, I posed that question to their supervisor during trial prep. As you now know, in the summer between high school graduation and the four years I served in the Navy, I worked at Union Carbide in Niagara Falls, N.Y. It was the norm for me and my co-workers to haul our filthy selves—the place was like working in a coal mine—to the bar across the street for lunch. The work was hard and dangerous, and we would normally have four eight-ounce beers and a shot of whiskey with our sandwich during our thirty-minute lunch.

The supervisor was a bit reluctant to talk with me about his men drinking on the job, but when I told him about my lunch hours at Union Carbide, he felt I wasn't just some "suit," and he spoke more freely. He asked me, "How much can you drink in half an hour, six or eight beers?" That's when I realized I was too much of a lightweight to have been an iron worker. Obviously, that story has stuck with me over the years.

I was fortunate to have had, at one point in time, an excellent prosecutor as my trial partner. He was extremely competent, quick thinking on his feet, witty as hell in a court room, and a master of practical jokes. We became particularly good friends.

Some of the lines he used with jurors that became my favorites were: "Trying to get that witness to give an honest answer to my question was like trying to nail Jello to a wall"; "Weighing the State's evidence against what the defense told you in this case is like comparing an anvil to a feather"; "When defense counsel told you that, it was the biggest understatement since Noah said, 'It looks like rain.'" And these are just a few.

It is not often that a prosecutor has the luxury of fingerprint evidence in a case. In fact, it is so rare that in one case my partner tried, the veteran detective being called to testify had never been able to bring fingerprint evidence to trial in his entire thirty-year career. And the detective was going to make the most of it. He prepared all sorts of charts and diagrams, and he was ready to give the jury a course in Fingerprints 101, which included the history of fingerprints.

There is only one thing that can hurt a prosecutor's case worse than a reluctant witness, and that is an exuberant witness who is difficult to control. This detective took the witness stand with paraphernalia in tow, and his nonresponsive first answer began with telling the jury how fingerprints may be intrinsically linked to drawings made by cavemen in cave dwellings during the Stone Age. The defense objected, and without missing a beat, my friend said, "Would you mind moving forward a few million years, Detective?" That response not only won him points with the jury, but it also focused the detective's testimony on how the fingerprints were important evidence in the case. I had a good laugh right along with the jury, the judge, and even the defendant.

There is one witness who I will always remember, whose circumstances and responses were memorable not because they humorous, but because of how the witness defied my preconceived notions. This gentleman was an eyewitness to a strong-arm robbery of an elderly couple on the Atlantic City Boardwalk. He gave police a detailed description of the incident and perpetrator.

A strong-arm robbery is one in which force, as opposed to a weapon, is used to accomplish a theft from the victim's person. Upon my initial review, the case looked strong except for the fact that the eyewitness was listed in police reports as homeless. Atlantic City, like most American cities, has a substantial homeless population. This wasn't the first or the last time I had a case with a homeless witness, and my detective and I began our search for him at the Atlantic City Rescue Mission.

If we were lucky, he was a resident there. I say "lucky" because most residents of the Mission did not want to speak with anyone from law enforcement who was looking for someone else, fearing they might reveal their own identity and be arrested on open charges or failure to appear for court warrants. Striking out at the Mission, we went to the next place we might find this witness or someone who knew him—under the Boardwalk itself.

At the time, there was quite the homeless encampment there, and it was a place where much unusual and illegal activity occurred. As such, it was not a safe place to be unless, like me, you were escorted by an armed detective. We had some success in that we spoke with someone who knew our witness and told us he would pass our business card on to the witness when he saw him again.

Much to our amazement, the very next day we received a phone call from the witness, saying we could meet him on the Boardwalk that afternoon to discuss the case. I was pleasantly surprised when we met him. He was articulate, accurate, and consistent in relaying details of the robbery to us. Additionally, he said he would keep in contact with us in the event we needed him to testify at trial.

He seemed different than the usual homeless people I encountered, and because my curiosity got the best of me, I asked him how he became homeless. He told me he'd previously run a successful business and lived in a beautiful home with his wife and daughter who meant more to him in life than anything else. When his wife and daughter were tragically killed in a car accident, he had a "breakdown," which left him suffering terribly from depression, and he "just walked away from everything." His explanation reminded me of what I had witnessed many times throughout my career. Sometimes very bad things happen to very good people.

It is not often that a prosecutor is pleasantly surprised by the response a lay (not law enforcement) prosecution witness gives to defense counsel's question on cross-examination. But it does occasionally happen.

I remember this occurring during a trial for a murder case where defense counsel was proposing to the jury that the witness, as opposed his client, was the real killer.

The witness's sister had been living with the defendant. On the day of the murder, the defendant borrowed the witness's car and drove it to a meeting with the victim, who had burned him in a drug deal by "shorting" him—selling him less cocaine than was negotiated. The meeting went badly and the defendant, as he later told the witness, "twisted his cap" (shot the victim in the head). The defendant then loaded the victim's body in the car's trunk, driving the car and body around all day waiting for the darkness of night to dispose of it.

While waiting for nightfall, the defendant enlisted the witness's help in attempting to destroy some of the victim's clothing and personal effects. Once it was dark, the witness helped the defendant dump the victim's body along power-lines in a densely wooded area.

The body was found the next morning—about one mile from my home. Coincidentally, I had changed my driving route to work that morning because of the police activity in the area.

Anyway, the witness fled to New York fearing that the defendant, who was a lieutenant in the Crips, would kill him next because of what he knew about the murder. A coworker of the witness also became aware of the killing because it took place in his front yard. When he and the witness went there to eat lunch, they found a copious amount of blood, the victim's skull fragments, and some of his teeth.

The witness then told his coworker that he'd had a conversation with the defendant who described what had occurred. Later that evening, the coworker's conscience got the best of him, and he went with his lawyer to the local police department to tell them what he knew.

Police began searching for the witness, and eventually he was persuaded to return to Atlantic County by a detective who knew him. When he arrived back in the county, he was arrested by Prosecutor's Office Major Crime Squad (MCS) detectives and charged with obstructing justice, destroying evidence, and improperly disposing of human remains.

He waived his Constitutional right to remain silent and agreed to answer the MCS detectives' questions. After hours of posturing and numerous different stories, he finally came clean with information about the murder. He was then taken to the county jail where he remained for the period it took him to make bail.

At trial, the defense offered several witnesses who had pending charges to testify that the witness had admitted to them that he shot the victim. Most of these witnesses had prior criminal records, and it was easy for me to refute their testimony on cross-examination, not only with their prior criminal history, but also the fact that they would like to "stick it" to the prosecution because of pending charges.

I know that I have segued a bit from the witness's testimony, but you needed background information to see why I was so pleased with his response to a single question. When he was asked, "Isn't it true that you told other inmates at the jail while you were incarcerated, that you and not my client shot the victim?" I expected him to say, as someone with a criminal record who was no stranger to the prison system would, that you don't talk about your case with other inmates because they might take that information to the prosecutor as a bargaining chip to lighten their sentence.

That answer really would not have helped my case since he was getting a reduced sentence because of his cooperation. Instead, he gave what I considered to be the perfect answer, and one which totally surprised me. His response was, "No, because I didn't do it."

As a postscript to the story, this defendant remained a fugitive for some eighteen months and killed two other people during this time. One killing occurred in Texas and the other in Georgia. By law, those two murders could not be used as evidence at his trial because they would have prejudiced the jury.

You may remember from a previous chapter about judges that I discussed a case in which I was nearly held in contempt of court. One of the three shooters in that case had a minimal record, making it difficult for me to damage to his credibility during testimony.

His defense was that he was present but misidentified as a participant in the shooting. When questioned by his attorney on direct examination, he told the jury that he had been to that restaurant many times because he was fond of the batter-dipped chicken on the menu.

As part of my case, I had a diagram prepared of the

restaurant and parking area. I began my cross-examination by showing him the diagram and asking him if he acknowledged it as being accurate. He said that he did not. From his very first response to my question, it was obvious to me that he wanted to fence, avoiding confirmation of even the most innocuous facts. That wasn't going to score any points with the jury, especially after hearing the judge explain in final jury instructions that they must consider whether the witness was evasive, hesitant, or reluctant in answering questions from either party.

I asked him to reaffirm whether he'd just told the jury that he had been there many times because he liked the batter-dipped chicken. He admitted he had. Using this line of questioning to show his reluctance to answer my questions, I asked, "And despite the fact that you've been there maybe hundreds of times, you dispute that diagram accurately shows the restaurant and parking lot?" He said, "Well not hundreds, but maybe a hundred, and yes to your question."

I told him that we would try it a different way. I asked, "Weren't you present in the courtroom last week when the owner of the restaurant testified that the diagram accurately shows the premises?" He said he was. I then asked if, considering the owner's testimony, was he still willing to tell the jury that the diagram was not accurate. He answered, "Yes, because I ain't never seen it from no helicopter before."

His response elicited so much laughter from the jury that I almost sent it to Reader's Digest. I could go on for some time reminiscing about certain witnesses and will return to this topic repeatedly in future chapters.

YOU TAKE THEM AS YOU FIND THEM

MANY TIMES, THE PROSECUTION FINDS that the victim or witnesses in a case are as unsavory as the criminal defendant. In those cases, often you hear these types of statements from the prosecution in its opening and closing arguments:

- "I didn't select this victim or these witnesses, the defendant gave them to you in committing the crime";
- "In preparing for this trial, I wasn't able to go to central casting, and select the victim or witnesses. This isn't theater, it's reality";
- "Members of the jury, you don't find swans in a sewer"; or
- "If I had a choice, I probably would have selected more polished witnesses than you saw, but the fact is their testimony is totally corroborated by the other evidence in the case."

These patent statements sometimes were not enough, and as a prosecutor, you might have to go deeper into apologizing for your witnesses, or simply get lucky. As with anything else, luck is often better than skill.

Any prosecutor will tell you that the worst time to try cases is the weeks leading up to Thanksgiving or Christmas. Like most people, jurors tend to be more generous around the holidays. If forced to try a case, a prosecutor would: choose a more minor case where there was less riding on the outcome; select a case which had strong and compelling evidence; or pick a case where the victim's circumstances are more pathetic than the defendant's, to make the victim more likable to the jury.

A case with all three elements present would be ideal. Unfortunately, that's seldom an option.

On one occasion, I knew that the judge was anxious to try a case two weeks before Thanksgiving. The end of the calendar year was near, and it was important for him to get as many trials as possible for statistical purposes. This judge had tried many cases that year, but between all the judges there was a competition to try the most. I also knew the case he would select. The defendant had been incarcerated for some time pending trial, and those cases are prioritized—rightfully so.

The defendant and victim in the case worked together in an old rooming house in Atlantic City that was being remodeled. They got into an argument, and the victim threw the defendant down a flight of stairs. They were both similar in stature, but the defendant was overpowered, probably because he had a prosthetic leg.

Later that day, the victim was waiting at a bus stop when the defendant approached him and, seeking revenge, attempted to plunge a knife into the victim's chest. The day was cold and the victim, who was wearing gloves, got his hand up attempting to defend himself. The knife went completely through his hand.

Bystanders witnessed the stabbing, and the defendant was arrested by police a short time later. The victim and defendant both had substantial criminal records, but because the defendant did not testify, the jury only heard about the victim's criminal convictions from defense counsel, who effectively used them during cross-examination to attack his credibility.

The morning I was to deliver my closing argument, I was telling my wife what a difficult task it would be to persuade the jury to convict, since the victim was more unlikeable than the defendant. She agreed and wished me luck. In a criminal case, the defense sums up first.

This defendant was represented by a public defender who was an excellent trial lawyer. To this day, I marvel at the number of indignant defendants who, when told by a judge that they should apply for a public defender, responded, "I don't want a public defender. I want a real lawyer." The Atlantic County Office of the Public Defender was staffed with exceptional attorneys who tried some of the most serious cases.

The public defender in this case was doing a terrific job summing up to a "quasi-self-defense" defense. As I sat there listening, I heard an opening. Defense counsel said, "I'm not asking you to like my client, nor am I asking you to invite him to Thanksgiving dinner, but he has rights within the law like anyone else, and among those rights is the right to defend himself." My closing argument began with: "Let's assume defense counsel, myself, you members of the jury, and the defendant would be invited to Thanksgiving dinner. I think all but one of us would agree who we would not give the knife when it came time to carve the turkey." The jury and even the judge got a good chuckle from that line, and the jury convicted the defendant after less than an hour of deliberations. A prosecutor often takes the victim and witnesses as he finds them, and sometimes gets lucky.

MEDICAL EXAMINERS AND OTHER FORENSIC PATHOLOGISTS

FORENSIC PATHOLOGISTS ARE MEDICAL DOCTORS who investigate "unexpected, suspicious, unnatural, and or violent deaths." "Forensic" is simply defined as "relating to courts of law." In New Jersey, all medical examiners are forensic pathologists paid by the state to determine cause and manner of death. Cause of death can vary. One example would be blunt force trauma to the head causing cerebral hemorrhaging. There are five manners of death: natural, accidental, suicide, homicide, and undetermined. In establishing cause and manner of death, the medical examiner will autopsy the deceased's body.

This procedure involves doing an external examination of the body for any injury, internally examining the body by removing and examining internal organs for injury or abnormality and collecting bodily fluids for toxicological screening.

During the internal examination, the medical examiner saws through and removes the deceased's skull cap. The brain is then removed, weighed, and visually examined. A "Y" incision is made on the deceased's chest, and a visual inspection for injuries or abnormalities is conducted before each vital organ is removed, weighed, and examined further. Tissue samples are taken and preserved for further microscopic examination. Every autopsy also includes examining stomach contents. The medical examiner carefully documents every step of the procedure. MCS detectives attend the autopsy when the death is suspicious and are there for the purpose of documenting and photographing it. All this is done with an eye toward testifying at a future trial.

During my career, the medical examiners were hired and paid by the county. The pay was not great considering the fact they were all doctors. Consequently, some were better than others, but all were characters. Some of my most interesting career memories relate to trial preparation with the medical examiners.

Other memorable moments came from encounters with defense forensic pathologists hired as expert witnesses to challenge the findings of the medical examiner. An expert witness can be called by either side when the expert's testimony will help a jury understand the evidence or determine a fact in issue. Because of their special knowledge, an expert witness can testify in the form of an opinion.

I worked with two different medical examiners during my career. Let me start by saying they were genuinely nice people whose gallows humor amused me every time we collaborated on a case.

The first medical examiner I will talk about was small in stature, and had a pleasing disposition, which made her likeable to juries. She was always cordial. Each time we encountered one another she would extend her hand, causing me to ask whether she was coming from work and washed her hands. She would giggle before answering in the affirmative, and I would then shake her hand and tell her she must be coming from work because her hand was cold. That would cause her to giggle even more. She would occasionally giggle by habit during graphic testimony. My goal was to work out the giggles before she testified. In a bizarre homicide case, she testified as my witness, and the defense hired a nationally renowned forensic pathologist as an expert witness to rebut her findings.

The defendant in the case was serving a prison sentence in Indiana when he and the victim began corresponding. Upon his release, he and the victim married, and he moved to New Jersey. The victim was a large woman who had weighed well over three hundred pounds. The relationship became stormy after only a few months because of the defendant's interest in a coworker; being a lesbian, she was not at all interested in him.

Anyway, the defendant and victim got into an argument one evening over his interest in the coworker, and the next morning he called the police saying he found his wife dead. Their residence was an efficiency apartment in a former motel that had been converted into apartments. The victim was found naked, kneeling in a praying position next to her bed. The only visible external injury was a linear wound to her forehead. The medical examiner concluded that the victim's cause of death was a skull fracture due to blunt force trauma, and the manner of death was homicide.

When the case was assigned to me for prosecution, two seasoned MCS forensic detectives came to tell me that the case was "a leaky bag of shit." The duties of forensic detectives assigned to MCS include processing the crime scene for the purpose of collecting evidence and photographing the crime scene and autopsy. These two detectives were excellent at what they did, and I am forever grateful for all they taught me that allowed me to effectively try homicide cases.

In this case, they said I had my work cut out for me since the defense expert witness had coauthored a book that was essentially the Bible of forensic pathology. He was reputed to be one of the leading forensic pathologists in the United States. His review of the medical examiner's report, and the crime scene and autopsy photos, led him to conclude that the wound to the victim's forehead was minor and mostly likely caused by her falling and striking the edge of an end table. He also determined the cause of her death to be cardiac arrest, and that the manner was natural. The diametrically opposed positions of the two forensic pathologists necessitated a trial.

The best way to take on an expert witness of this stature is to start by reading any books or articles the witness published. It is important to understand that expert witnesses know much more than you can ever learn in the time you have to prepare for trial. The best you can do is familiarize yourself with any opinions previously expressed in the expert's writings, and hope the witness contradicts that opinion during trial testimony. I thought I was ready for this witness because I'd read his book twice and focused on the part dealing with blunt force trauma. I chose poorly.

The defendant did not testify at trial because his lengthy prior record could have been used to attack his credibility, but in a statement he made to police at the time of his arrest, he denied ever striking the victim. He said he was working all night, and when he found the victim, he inexplicably placed her in the praying position in which the police found her. No weapon was found in the apartment that could have logically caused the wound.

The defense expert was an "artful dodger" on the witness stand. I came at him directly with opinions he expressed in his book regarding blunt force trauma. He was so elusive that the judge at one point shouted at him to "just answer the question, Doctor." He knew how to work a jury, and at one point in his testimony said, "I see you thoroughly read my book. If I ever write a sequel, I may ask you to edit it." The expert told me after he concluded his testimony to contact him for dinner if I ever found myself in Brooklyn.

I chose poorly in preparing for trial because in focusing on blunt force trauma, I neglected to consider positional asphyxiation as a cause of death. This cause would have been supported by the victim's girth and the position the defendant admitted placing her in. While I doubt the expert would have conceded to it as causing the victim's death, it would have gotten the jury to at least question the expert's opinion as to whether the victim's death was natural or a homicide.

What bothered me most is that I knew the defense expert felt he had gotten one over on me. I vowed that if our paths crossed again, I would be even more ready for him. The jury found the defendant guilty of manslaughter. The verdict was just, given that the defense seriously challenged the prosecution's opinion as to cause and manner of death. He was sentenced as a persistent offender. This doubled his sentence.

Years later, the same expert forensic pathologist was hired to testify in a sexual assault case I prosecuted. You may remember the case since I discussed it in a previous chapter. To refresh your recollection, the victim was attacked in the common bathroom of a rooming house where she lived. The defendant, a serial rapist, was hiding in the bathtub behind a shower curtain. When she sat down on the toilet, he accosted her. The defendant shoved a scarf the victim was wearing into her mouth to silence her screams. He then penetrated her with his fingers and penis before sodomizing her with a quart beer bottle.

The opinion of the expert in this case was that the victim's description of what happened was not credible, since had the defendant shoved the scarf in her mouth like she said, she would have choked to death.

This time I was ready for him. My first question on cross-examination was, "Doctor, let me see if I understand all of this. The defense paid you $15,000 to come in here and say what the defendant did to her should have killed her?" He angrily shot back, "Money means nothing to me!" Hardly the answer jurors who were missing work and paid two dollars per day for jury service wanted to hear. From that point on, I asked questions that I knew he took personally, and he grew angrier.

An hour or so later, I had about finished my cross-examination, and as I walked back to my seat at counsel table, I thought to myself, "What the hell." I pulled a clean handkerchief from my pocket, had it marked for identification, and approached the witness stand. Two of my colleagues who were in the courtroom later told me they thought to themselves, "I really can't believe he's going to do it."

After getting him to admit he wasn't present when the crime was committed, and telling him that he could only speculate on the depth to which the defendant inserted the scarf into the victim's throat, I said, "Doctor, I am going to shove this handkerchief down my throat and I want you to tell me when I might die, because I still have a closing argument to deliver this afternoon." He was now furious, looked at the judge, and personally objected to my question. While he was objecting, I kept shoving the handkerchief in my mouth asking, "Now? Now?" The judge calmly said, "Just answer the question, Doctor." The jury loved it. We broke for lunch right after his testimony and I asked him whether the Brooklyn dinner invitation was still open. He told me to go fuck myself. I just gave him a big smile.

A reporter from the local newspaper was in the courtroom while all this was happening, and the next day he wrote an article about it using the byline, "Prosecutor tries to kill himself to make a point." Weeks later, a writer for the

American Bar Association Journal interviewed me about my
use of the handkerchief. He then wrote a short blurb about it
that appeared in the ABA Journal alongside other humorous
courtroom happenings.

The other medical examiner I worked with was truly
knowledgeable, but due to a language barrier, juries found it
difficult to understand him. When he was asked by one of my
colleagues during trial prep if he could clarify for the jury the
extent to which blunt force trauma caused injury to the homicide victim's brain, he responded, "Brain like radio. Drop radio
and outside looks good, but inside—whoaaa!" An interesting
analogy.

I always got a kick out of the fact that any time I met with
him for trial he would ask me at the outset, "Did he do it?"
I would always respond, "As a matter of fact, he did. That's
why we are here, Doc." Like most intellectuals I have met in
life, he was quite absent-minded. He was never prepared for
trial preparation; in fact, after asking "did he do it," he would
then spend the next ten minutes or so trying to locate his
file. When he found the file, it became obvious that he hadn't
looked at it since the autopsy, which was usually a year or two
prior. I tried four or five different homicide cases with him.
Each time we talked, it was like he was meeting me for the
first time.

On one occasion, a college intern accompanied my investigator and I to the medical examiner's office for trial preparation. The student was eager to learn, and on the drive over
asked what kind of witness we thought the medical examiner
would be at trial. I told him about the medical examiner's

absent mindedness and how he testified numerous times for me over the past couple of years. To illustrate the point, I told him to introduce himself as me and conduct the interview when we got there. The student was extremely nervous about it, but did play along for the first five minutes or so during our trial prep. When I saw the student could not go any further with the prank, I told the medical examiner what was going on. He did have a good sense of humor and laughed along with us.

In another trial prep meeting with him, I showed him an autopsy photograph of the victim's chest—clearly a male. It was a closeup taken of a fatal stab wound just below the victim's left nipple. He asked me whether the victim was a man or a woman. I told him that he must have dated only flat chested women in his life if he could not discern this victim's gender. He got a laugh out of that too.

As I understand it, this medical examiner was a collector of fine and expensive art. Years after he retired, he was hanging a painting in his home and fell off a stepladder. The fall was serious given his age. He will be missed. Cause of death: blunt force trauma to the head with cerebral hemorrhaging. Manner of death: accidental.

THE NAKED MAN CASE

THE CASE WITH THE MOST unusual set of facts I tried during my career had to have been "The Naked Man Case." I decided upon that name after each of the many witnesses I contacted on the case said, "You must be calling about the naked man case."

The defendant "naked man," a New York resident, stole a 1984 Volvo with New York license plates from a repair shop on Long Island, New York. He drove to the Trump Plaza Hotel/Casino in Atlantic City and parked in the parking garage. He went to the casino floor and began playing black-jack. At one point he was up $4,000, but within hours lost his winnings and any money he brought with him. He then left the casino floor, returned to the garage, and slept in the Volvo. The next day, he broke into several vehicles belonging to casino patrons and employees. The defendant then went to the Trump Taj Mahal Casino and broke into more vehicles there, stealing more property. On two occasions he had contact with the same Atlantic City police officer.

The items he stole included two registered handguns, a shotgun, and two registered rifles from different vehicles. He also took a suitcase that contained Valium prescribed for the owner.

The vehicle owners began reporting the thefts to casino security and the police.

A day later, the same ACPD officer who had previous contact with the defendant saw him acting strangely, and a description of the defendant was reported to the ACPD. While this was happening, the defendant drove the Volvo to a nearby casino dealer's school where he took New Jersey plates off a parked vehicle and switched them for the New York plates.

The following day, two ACPD bicycle patrol officers saw the defendant driving the Volvo from the direction of the Trump Plaza. It was filled with stolen property. When the officers attempted to pull the defendant over while he stopped at an intersection, the defendant made eye contact and then drove off and onto the Atlantic City Expressway. The bicycle officers broadcast the vehicle's description and its direction of travel over their radios.

Another uniformed ACPD patrol officer in a marked car heard the broadcast and saw the Volvo driving out of Atlantic City and onto the expressway. He activated his overhead lights and pulled the defendant over. The officer exited his marked vehicle, and with his weapon drawn, approached the Volvo. He ordered the defendant to turn off the motor, drop the keys out the window, and to keep his hands on the steering wheel. The defendant did not comply, instead choosing to drive off at high speed. The officer got back in his marked unit and gave chase while broadcasting his pursuit of the defendant over the radio.

A second ACPD officer heard the broadcast while pulled over on the shoulder of the expressway, monitoring the flow of traffic. When he looked in his rearview mirror, he saw the Volvo being driven on the shoulder at what he estimated to be forty miles per hour. This officer tried to pull off the shoulder, but his vehicle stalled, and the Volvo rammed into him. The force of the collision dislodged the bench seat in the police vehicle and propelled it forward, knocking the officer uncon-scious and causing other disabling injuries. The defendant, who was wearing black pants, a white shirt, work gloves, and a bandana, exited the Volvo, crossed the roadway, and entered a marshy area full of tall reeds and dune grass.

Canine units and a New Jersey State Police helicopter joined in the search for the defendant. About ninety minutes later, a canine patrol officer found the defendant lying in the mud naked and concealed under marsh grass. The defendant was told to stand, raise his hands, and interlock his fingers. He complied, was handcuffed, and placed under arrest. By now, a photographer from the local newspaper arrived on the scene, and as the naked, handcuffed defendant was being escorted out of the marsh by police, the photographer snapped a pho-tograph. The photo appeared on the front page of the newspa-per. It showed the naked defendant from the waist up because the reeds and marsh grass were just at the right height to cover his privates. The Naked Man case was born.

The saga does not end here. The defendant was transported

to the hospital for treatment of cuts and abrasions, and a blood sample was taken. Lab results showed the presence of Valium in his system.

Another ACPD officer transported the defendant from the hospital to police headquarters, but the defendant somehow managed to slip out of one handcuff en route. When they arrived at headquarters, the officer opened the door to help the defendant out of the police vehicle, and the defendant pushed the officer to the ground and fled. The officer broadcast what had just occurred, and another officer spotted the defendant and gave chase.

The defendant then swung and struck the approaching officer in the head. The officer tackled the defendant to the ground, and after a struggle, subdued him. That officer suffered a knee injury requiring surgery.

Plea negotiations in the case were protracted. The defendant could not deny that he committed the crimes because there were eyewitnesses to most of them. Instead, he claimed that he was so intoxicated that he was not aware of the nature of his actions or that they were wrong. Intoxication is an affirmative legal defense. He bootstrapped this assertion with his prior psychiatric history to allege his ability to determine right from wrong was diminished, and that he was suffering from a mental disease caused by cocaine abuse and dependence, which rendered him unable to know that what he was doing was wrong. This legal defense is referred to as diminished capacity.

The defendant hired two psychiatrists to testify at trial. He told them he was having auditory hallucinations at the time he broke into the vehicles in the casino garages. He denied taking the items for monetary purposes, but said he took them to silence voices he heard that were mocking him. He said these voices also urged him to flee the police. The defendant contended that he had little or no recollection of events that preceded his apprehension, attributing it to his intoxication and diminished capacity. He admitted to taking three or four Valium.

The prosecution hired its own psychiatrist to examine the defendant and to testify as to the validity of his intoxication and diminished capacity defenses. This psychiatrist was board-certified in addiction medicine. He rebutted one of the defense experts' assertions, opining that if the defendant suffered from chronic schizoaffective disorder, it was in remission. He also testified that the defendant was able to distinguish right from wrong. The defendant's "complex, goal-directed, purposeful acts required memory of the recent past, awareness of the present, and demonstrated an ability to anticipate future consequences and events." In other words, the defendant obviously fled from police because he knew what he did was wrong. The prosecution's expert witness also testified that any auditory or visual hallucinations the defendant experienced were not powerful enough to overcome "his knowing, purposeful, and goal-directed conduct."[1]

The testimony of the three expert psychiatrists was interesting and crucial to determining the defendant's guilt or

---

[1]For a more precise statement of the facts of the case and testimony of the expert witnesses, See State v. Bauman, 298 N.J. Super 176 (App. Div. 1997).

innocence. However, it was a small part of the total testimony given in the case, considering the number of police officers involved in the defendant's apprehension and the number of victims who had property stolen from their vehicles in the casino parking garages.

The most humorous testimony came from a victim from Arkansas who had had a shotgun and rifle stolen from his RV. When I handed him the shotgun for the purpose of identifying it as his, he took the weapon, caressed it, and with tears in in his eyes said, "that's my baby." When I handed him the rifle, he identified it as belonging to his wife. He said, "She don't hunt or nothin'. She just uses it to shoot racoons in the ass to keep them out of the trash cans." The jury was quite amused.

The defendant was found guilty on most of the many charges and received a lengthy sentence. His conviction was affirmed on appeal. Eventually, the naked truth was exposed.

LET'S GO TO THE VIDEOTAPE

IT WAS BOUND TO HAPPEN. In the interest of saving money and staying up to date, New Jersey courtrooms eliminated court reporters, often referred to as stenographers. Trial lawyers on both sides lost a great ally with this decision; court reporters were a tremendous asset in a trial. Meticulously recording every word while also observing the reaction of jurors, their feedback provided helpful insight into how your trial strategy was being received by the twelve people who mattered most. While transitioning to video came at great cost, video recordings provided a powerful weapon to attorneys who knew how to use it effectively.

There was nothing more persuasive than standing before a jury with a transcript in hand during summation and telling them that, memorialized in this "official record" of the proceeding, the witness said exactly X. While this was an effective technique, it still did not capture the raw emotion normally associated with the actual testimony, nor did it fully demonstrate the body language of an evasive witness avoiding the truth. Certainly, not like playing the video portion of the testimony does. This was particularly true when jurors asked for a readback of certain testimony during deliberations, and a court reporter read the testimony to the jury in a monotone voice to avoid emphasizing any part of it. Videotape playbacks gave jurors the opportunity to see the trial twice.

During my first run in with videotaped testimony, I was fortunate to be accompanied by the most knowledgeable judge on substantive and procedural law in the entire state. He was a judge who rewarded creativity, and he allowed me to use the video recording, saying that it was no different from a transcript because it was the official record of the proceeding. Using the video recording required a lot of work.

Unlike a typewritten transcript where you skim the entirety of it to find exactly what you need, picking and choosing from a video requires recalling what the witness said and precisely when they said it. In some cases, you needed to watch hours of testimony to find minutes for use in summation. That part was easy. The difficult part for me was "extracting" that testimony from the whole trial and making a highlight video capturing exactly and only what the jury should see. Primarily, it required two VCRs and the technical ability to record with precision. Lacking the latter, I turned to the most supportive champion of my career who is also exceptionally skilled at making these highlight tapes: my wife. She was truly the videographer in our family, who captured the memories we have of our now adult children.

As you can imagine, there is a certain amount of

gamesmanship that goes into any trial. While the rules of criminal procedure in New Jersey prohibit "trial by ambush"— the prosecution must provide the defense with all evidence it will use—during summation the prosecution gets a more level playing field in that it speaks last and does not need to disclose to the defense what will be said about evidence in the case.

The first time I used a videotape was during summation in a homicide case. The defense counsel was trying to convince the jury that his client stabbed his ex-wife to death in the heat of passion, rather than in a cold, calculated matter. When I played the testimony back, the defense attorney was caught unaware and went ballistic. In fact, his lengthy overreaction to the videotape of the defendant's testimony did more to persuade the jury than showing them that portion of testimony itself. It was at that moment that I was convinced prosecutors had a new secret weapon.

The next time I used a "highlight" tape was several months later in a sexual assault case. By now, word was spreading about how effective a summation tool it was. In this trial, the defense counsel thought he would try his hand at it, but it was immediately obvious that he did not do the leg work required in perfecting the method—because he did not have my wife assist him in preparing it. Instead of making a "highlight reel" from the original trial tape, he thought that he would narrow down that portion of the victim's testimony from the original and asked the court clerk to play it for him.

Unfortunately, it was not exactly what he had hoped for. What was shown was him appearing to badger the victim by asking how long individual aspects of the attack took, and her repeating, "I don't know, I wasn't looking at my watch. He was raping me." To make matters worse for the defendant, his counsel kept telling the clerk, "No, no that's not what I wanted." Obviously, this new weapon was even more dangerous in the wrong hands.

The summation highlight tape became a staple among my colleagues. I can only estimate the number of evenings and weekends they spent in my living room as my wife assisted in preparing their closing arguments. To this day, I tell her how she singlehandedly changed the case law addressing "video summations" in New Jersey. None of the cases in which these tapes were used was reversed on appeal. However, because New Jersey is a "progressive" state, it did not take long for the state's appellate courts to recognize how powerful this new tool was, and they quickly moved to limit their use.

As previously stated, because it was the court itself that decided to switch to videotaped proceedings, the argument could not be made that the video was anything but the official record. The first case reviewed on appeal required the prosecution to play the entire testimony, both direct and cross-examination, of the portion sought to be used for the jury. This prevented "cherry-picking," and the videos still had value from a prosecutor's perspective because a jury would hear the testimony twice.

As the case law progressed, the prosecutor now had to disclose a portion of summation to the defense by providing a copy of any videotaped testimony intended to be played in closing and allow the defense counsel to review it. Finally, the decision was made that only stenographic recordings would be used in homicide cases. I dedicate this chapter to my wife, and to my colleagues whose hard work made all this appellate review necessary.

THE CSI EFFECT

MOST PEOPLE ENJOY WATCHING TELEVISION crime shows, and let me start by saying that I also enjoy them, my favorite being *Law and Order*. I often watched looking for material from the writers to use in my closing arguments. While I seldom got the chance to use any of it, I clearly remember a line D.A. Jack McCoy used in an episode where a prostitute was sexually assaulted. In support of her credibility he said, "Putting a 'for sale' sign on a car parked on your front lawn is not an invitation to steal it." I never used that line because I never tried a sexual assault case where the victim was a prostitute.

But the rise in popularity of crime shows came with a problem: many people bring what they see on those shows with them to jury duty. They think the forensic science portrayed is real and expect to see satellite photos of the crime being committed, clear surveillance camera footage catching the perpetrator in the act, sketch artist's rendition of the accused, facial recognition technology establishing the defendant as the doer, gunpowder residue evidence in shoot-ing cases, DNA evidence in all sexual assault cases, and fin-gerprint evidence.

When watching a crime show, the commission of the crime, its investigation, apprehension, and the prosecution of the defendant fits neatly into a sixty-minute television seg-ment, including commercials. The reason for this is the events and forensic evidence portrayed are fictional. Jurors seldom saw it that way. The television crime shows created an obstacle to conviction prosecutors referred to as "the CSI effect."

At some point in my career, I began to feel common sense among jurors was becoming uncommon. Jurors were hanging cases where the defense counsel argued a failure by the prose-cution to present specific forensic evidence. For example: The police witness a defendant on a street corner in a hand-to-hand exchange of a small object for cash, and then seized a baggie of cocaine from the other person. However, the defense counsel then argued that the police failed to test the baggie for fingerprints, which would have conclusively proven that it was the item the defendant exchanged.

As hung (non-unanimous) juries became more frequent, requiring my colleagues and me to either reduce plea offers or retry cases, we began to go on the offensive in dealing with the CSI effect. Sometimes it simply required asking additional questions of the officer, like in the case above. On that occa-sion, the officer explained that drugs packaged for resale pass through many hands and the likelihood of finding "usable" fingerprints for comparison purposes was remote. In rebut-ting the defendant's lack of fingerprint evidence, a prosecutor might also argue that fingerprint evidence is important in locating a suspect. In this case, the officer witnessed the crime being committed.

Other times it required calling and qualifying a fingerprint expert witness to explain the absence of fingerprint evidence. The expert would explain that fingerprints appear on a surface when oils secreted from the skin contact that surface. If a person is a non-secretor, no latent fingerprints will be left. Temperature, moisture, and humidity all seriously affect the possibility of finding usable prints for comparison purposes.

The type of surface also affects whether fingerprints will be found. Flat, smooth surfaces are more likely to produce fingerprint evidence; rough surfaces rarely reveal such evidence. For example, fingerprint evidence is seldom if ever found on a handgun. The grip on a handgun is raised, making it impossible to find fingerprint evidence. Additionally, the barrel of a handgun is oily and the chemical interaction with the skin significantly reduces the possibility of finding fingerprints. Finally, fingerprints are not time-stamped. They could have been left yesterday or six months ago depending on environmental conditions.

Latent fingerprints found on an item need to be matched with known fingerprints. In other words, if police find fingerprint evidence in searching for a suspect, but that person's fingerprints are not on file somewhere, no comparison can be made, and that person will remain at large. Fingerprint evidence is rare, and only one of the thousands of cases I prosecuted involved fingerprint evidence.

DNA evidence is conclusive in identifying a defendant

as a source, but not always available. If a sexual assault victim bathes before being examined for forensic evidence, it is unlikely that DNA evidence will be found. When the victim is penetrated digitally, no bodily fluid is transferred from the defendant, so DNA evidence will be absent. Finally, DNA evidence does not negate a consent defense where there is no corroborating evidence.

Sometimes testing for gunpowder residue evidence is helpful; other times, it isn't. If a shooter thoroughly washes his hands after firing a weapon, the chances of finding gunpowder residue is remote. When a handgun is fired, the gases caused by the explosion propelling the projectile carry some gunpowder residue. A person standing near the shooter and the victim may have gunpowder residue on them even though they never fired the gun.

Facial recognition technology was not around before I retired, and I only had one case where a police sketch artist prepared a drawing of the suspect. In that prosecution, the sketch was a good likeness of the defendant. The witness's perceptive ability in combination with the trauma caused by witnessing the event often determines the degree of similarity between the sketch and the accused.

Often, a witness or victim knew the accused. These situations lighten the prosecutor's burden of proving beyond a reasonable doubt that the defendant was the perpetrator. Stranger-on-stranger crimes presented a greater challenge, and identification of the defendant was usually accomplished through either an in-person (show up) procedure or a photographic lineup. In these cases, a prosecutor might argue that the trauma caused by the event "etched the defendant's face in the victim's memory."

A prosecutor might also emphasize parts of the judge's final jury instructions on how to determine the accuracy of the witness's identification of the defendant. To bolster credibility, the prosecutor would say the witness had ample time to observe the defendant while the crime was being committed; the positive identification was conclusive and made without hesitation; and the identification procedure was conducted fairly without any suggestion from the police as to who to select.

Videotaped evidence can be a blessing or a curse. I once had a case where the defendant was stealing the stereo from a car parked in a casino parking garage. The victim was returning to his car and caught the defendant in the act. The defendant then turned on the victim, stabbing him in the face with the screwdriver used to remove the stereo. These actions turned a simple auto burglary into an armed robbery.

I thought the prosecution would be open and shut since the incident must have been recorded on surveillance cameras; Atlantic City casinos have many surveillance cameras on property. I asked my investigator to retrieve the videotape from the parking garage. I reviewed the tape and, much to my chagrin, it did not show the incident at all.

Rather, the camera singly focused on the curb just outside the elevator entrance to that level. The casino had been confronted with several lawsuits from patrons who falsely claimed to have fallen at that same location. The camera was being used to record and refute these phony claims. The defendant pled guilty and casino security was able to avoid embarrassing trial testimony.

Another case I prosecuted involved a homicide where the victim was shot point blank in the head. The murder occurred late at night on the sidewalk across the street from a warehouse. Surveillance footage from the warehouse showed the incident from start to finish, but it was so dark and grainy that faces were unrecognizable. However, the defendant was short and had an awkward body shape that made him distinguishable on the tape. Other circumstantial evidence in the case pointed to him as the shooter and he eventually pleaded guilty to murder.

The CSI effect was a creative way for the defense to challenge the prosecution's case, often requiring the prosecution to prove a negative, which is not easy to do. Sometimes it worked for the defense and sometimes it did not, but the prosecution always needed to address it.

CONFLICTED

I WAS OCCASIONALLY ASSIGNED A case because other attorneys in the office could not prosecute it due to a conflict they had with a defendant or witness. I refer to this situation as being conflicted into a case. Other times, a case that you were prosecuting had to be reassigned because of certain conflicts, real or imaginary, that existed between yourself and the defendant or a witness in the case. I will refer to this situation as being conflicted out of a case.

There are instances of each that remain etched in my mind, and ironically, both involved allegations of misconduct by me. I use the term "ironic" because I had nothing to do with being conflicted in or out of either case.

No prosecutor in the office was required to join the Atlantic County Bar Association. To me, membership was reserved for those whose aspirations were to become a superior court judge. Additionally, there was a feeling among some prosecutors and public defenders that civil practitioners looked upon us as inferior lawyers because our work was not about money. I had no desire to become a judge and chose not to spend money to belong to a group solely motivated by it.

My failure to join the County Bar Association is what got me conflicted into a certain case. In the case, a member of the county bar was alleged to have assaulted someone. The alleged victim was intoxicated and had no recollection of specific facts. It was my job to determine whether the case should go forward. As always, I was ethically bound not to pursue any case that could not be proved beyond a reasonable doubt.

The person allegedly assaulted had been drinking all day. He left a bar late at night and encountered the accused, who was with a female companion. Words were exchanged and then blows. Photos taken at the scene depicted a bloody encounter where the alleged victim suffered serious injuries that were exacerbated by a preexisting condition. There were no witnesses to the incident other than the accused, his female companion, and the alleged victim.

The accused went to the police after knowing that the incident was being investigated. A statement from the female companion submitted by counsel representing the accused said the accused acted in self-defense. Once again, the alleged victim could provide no details of the encounter.

The alleged victim was represented by a prominent law firm, and a lawyer from the firm, who was a former attorney general, shadowed me during my investigation of the case. The firm represented the alleged victim in a civil suit he was pursuing against the accused.

My investigation began at the bar the alleged victim left shortly before the encounter. Police indicated in reports that they had seized a video depicting an area near the bar, but it was not useful since the incident happened off camera. I talked with the bartender who was working on the night of the incident. She recalled the alleged victim being in the crowded bar, that he'd been intoxicated and "hitting on her." She said his comments were "nothing out of the ordinary" compared to what she usually encountered from customers.

I next visited the alleged victim and his sister. She had spent the day with him. He again recalled nothing further of the incident. The sister was not present when the incident occurred but opined that the alleged victim had to have been attacked.

As part of the investigation, I spoke with a police officer who interviewed the accused when he surrendered to police hours after the incident. The officer said that he confronted the accused with the fact that police had seized a video showing the encounter (false but not illegal). The accused became teary-eyed and asked if he was in trouble.

Given both the severity of the injuries to the alleged victim, and the paucity of evidence, I decided to present the case to a grand jury for their determination as to whether probable cause existed to indict the accused.

The cliché that a prosecutor "can indict a ham sandwich" if he or she chooses is true. The reason being that the grand jury only hears the prosecution's side of the evidence. My goal here was to fairly present the case and not steer the grand jury in one direction or another.

When I candidly told the former attorney general what I intended to do he was livid. He insulted me by asking if I was afraid to try the case. Had he taken the time to ask any judge or defense attorney in the courthouse that question, he might not have been ignorant enough to insult me with it. He also suggested that his client was being "home cooked" because he did not reside in the area. Ignorant comment number two.

He accompanied his client to my office on the day scheduled for grand jury, angrily insisting that he be present while I prepared the alleged victim to testify. Now he was going too far. After asking his client to step out of the room, I told the attorney that he had seconds to leave or I would have my investigator, who was also present, "cuff him and drag him out." He got the message, and knowing he had no legal right to sit in, left upon his own accord.

The grand jury voted not to indict the accused after being presented with all the facts. The former attorney general filed an abuse of discretion complaint with the Attorney General's Office alleging that I had not properly handled the case. The complaint was dismissed.

In contrast, the case I was conflicted out of had plenty of evidence. The two defendants in the case were notorious for committing burglaries on commercial establishments throughout the county. In addition to committing break-ins together, they also happened to be brothers.

These defendants would choose a business that was closed for the day, disarm the alarm system, climb up to the roof, and cut a hole in it to lower themselves down into the premises. They weren't particular and broke into all kinds of businesses, ranging from laundromats to restaurants. The damage they caused breaking into the establishment usually exceeded the value of the property they stole. Quite often they would simply break into a vending machine and take whatever coins it contained.

Law enforcement authorities throughout the county had a good idea that it was these two brothers committing the burglaries, but they needed to catch them in the act. The burglaries became so numerous that a county task force was formed to do just that.

Officers set up rooftop surveillance during many cold nights that winter, spending hours at separate locations in hopes that the pair would strike there next. After months of conducting this operation, the two defendants picked the wrong target and were arrested. They were charged with some twenty different burglaries, all committed in the same manner. To this day, these two defendants remind me of the "wet bandits" from the Christmas movie *Home Alone*.

My plea offer to both called for a lengthy prison sentence. They each had extensive criminal records, the crimes they were charged with were numerous, and the evidence was strong. Those are the three most principal factors in determining an appropriate plea offer.

The case dragged on for months as defense counsel tried to persuade me to significantly reduce the plea offer. Other things that factored into the plea offer were that substantial law enforcement resources were expended catching these two guys, and most of the victims owned mom-and-pop businesses that lost considerable revenue because of the break-ins. I stood fast on my offer.

Shortly before the matter was given a date for trial, one

of the defendants wrote a letter to the county prosecutor demanding that I be removed from the case because of a conflict. In the letter, he stated that I had an argument with him while picking my young son up from a birthday party for a classmate. The defendant alleged that I was abusing my discretion in treating him harshly because of this prior encounter. Even though this never happened, the prosecutor was duty bound to turn the matter over to the attorney general for investigation, and I was removed from the case.

As part of the attorney general's investigation, I was required to submit a sworn statement refuting the burglar's allegations. That was easy because I was out-of-state on the date this was alleged to have happened. I do have a son, but the burglar had gotten his name completely wrong, and I did not own the type of vehicle the defendant said I was driving.

To his credit, the defendant got the break he and his brother were seeking. The much less experienced prosecutor assigned to the case after my removal pled the case for what can only be described as a "sweet deal" for the pair. I was eventually cleared of any wrongdoing by the attorney general, but it did take me a while to get over the lenient plea recommendation of my colleague. The police officers who spent nights on various rooftops were especially pissed.

It is fair to say that this imaginary conflict the burglar had cooked up had very real consequences.

ACPD DECOY ROBBERY UNIT

THE MEMBERS OF THE ACPD Decoy Robbery Unit consisted of the most creative, courageous, and proactive police officers I worked with during my career as a prosecutor. The unit was the brainchild of Detective Ron Lane and comprised of five officers, all of whom, including Captain Larry Ross, could only be described as "cops' cops." These officers worked as a team to take violent criminals who posed a threat to Atlantic City's tourists off the streets.

Detective Lane was the main cog in this well-oiled machine. He would dress to appear as a "nerdy" drunken tourist who lost his way, only to find himself in a hopelessly dangerous situation within blocks of the casinos. The unit strategically chose the most isolated areas to stage their operation to give the criminals confidence that they would not be detected. Little did they know that the unit chose the locations because they offered limited means of escape for the robbers. In other words, the predators became the prey.

Each incident was taped by an officer specifically assigned to that duty. The other officers concealed themselves at a distance where they could observe Detective Lane and move in as quickly as possible to apprehend the robbers before they could harm him. The unit was not as concerned with criminals who would simply try to pickpocket Lane or talk him into giving up his cash. Rather, the officers focused on apprehending those persons who used force or threatened Lane with a weapon.

As you can imagine, this posed great danger to Lane, who on separate occasions had a knife placed to his throat, and often sustained injuries requiring treatment in the ER. Additionally, other officers suffered substantial injury while apprehending those robbers who often violently resisted. To further add to the danger, on nights the unit set up operation, other patrol officers were told at rollcall to avoid the area so as not to dissuade any "would be" robbers. On many occasions, the unit would have been legally justified in using deadly force to protect Lane, but they did not resort to it. This was a fact the unit was proud of.

The unit was extremely successful. In the year or so that the operation was conducted, one hundred and twenty-five arrests were made, all resulting in conviction. Every ten days, the unit would conduct the operation. The work was both physically and mentally taxing on the officers. There's no telling how many more arrests would have been made had the officers been physically able to operate more often.

I was in awe the first time I watched a video from one of the cases. Lane was approached no less than ten times in a single evening before the two robbers I was prosecuting threw him to the ground and began punching him. As they rifled through Lane's pockets, the team moved in, and a violent struggle ensued. I prosecuted many of the unit's cases, and the response of the robbers was always, "I had no idea he was a cop." A tribute to how persuasive Lane was in his role, and how well orchestrated the unit worked together as a team.

The unit gained such notoriety that the nationally televised show *20/20* did a piece on them. I was flattered when Captain Ross asked me to appear with them on the show, but I needed permission to appear. That permission was denied because my appearance would have painted Atlantic City "in a bad light." It was my opinion that if anything, the broadcast showed what lengths these courageous Atlantic City police officers went in protecting visitors and other members of the community.

The officers who spoke on the show did an excellent job of explaining how the operation worked and its success. I recall the interviewer seeming to suggest that this might be a form of entrapment, but entrapment is only a defense if, but for the actions of police, the defendant would not have committed the crime. It was obvious that these robbers were intent on finding and then robbing a vulnerable victim, especially since the robbers had no other reason to be in the areas where the unit conducted its operation.

The Decoy Robbery Unit performed its duties admirably in reducing the number of robberies in the tourism district. They went beyond what the job requires in terms of placing themselves in harm's way to protect others. It was a privilege to prosecute the cases they made and an honor to know and have worked with them.

TRYING TO STOP THE KILLING

EARLIER, I COMMENTED ABOUT WITNESSES who were reluctant to testify for one of two reasons. Either they feared retaliation by the defendant or sought retribution outside of what was occurring in a courtroom. The second situation was more dangerous in that it often led to more killing. As a prosecutor, you needed to recognize these situations and take available legal measures to ensure that these witnesses testified at trial.

Many times, this entailed simply moving a witness to another county jail to avoid contact between the witness and defendant. More rarely, it was necessary to move a witness to another county or state. Despite what television and movies portray, this situation was the exception rather than the rule. Only once in my twenty-five-year career did it become necessary to relocate a witness.

The witness in that case was an eyewitness to a homicide. The victim was gunned down in the courtyard of a public housing project where the eyewitness resided. She saw the killing from several feet away while looking out her kitchen window. The defendant was a local guy who was known to most people residing in the housing project. The first time I met the witness, she was reluctant but seemed unafraid to testify.

The night before she was to testify, she frantically called my trial detective saying that the front of her apartment was "shot up." ACPD officers and MCS detectives responded to her call and observed the outside front wall of her apartment to be riddled with bullet holes.

She appeared distraught and said she was not going to testify unless she was relocated to another residence. There were limited funds for relocating witnesses, and the greater part of the evening was spent preparing and getting approvals on the necessary paperwork. The witness spent that night in a secure location under the protection of MCS detectives.

She testified the next morning and was given a voucher to be used for relocation expenses. We learned weeks after the trial concluded that she moved to a newer housing project just blocks away. Further investigation by the ACPD revealed that an acquaintance of the witness was responsible for firing shots into the front wall of her former apartment. She was using her testimony to acquire better accommodations. You never quite knew the difference between a witness trying to get one over on you, and a witness that genuinely feared retaliation, but it was always better to err on the side of caution.

The witnesses who sought retribution were usually driven. Most defendants charged with committing a homicide remain in jail pending trial, so quite often persons seeking retribution against an incarcerated defendant look to injure or kill someone close to the defendant. I once tried a homicide where the sole purpose of witnesses was just that.

In that case, persons associated with the victim sought to shoot the defendant's girlfriend as retribution. To that end, the shooter(s) went to the girlfriend's mother's house one night attempting to locate her. They lurked outside the home peering through windows. When they saw what appeared to be the girlfriend enter a bedroom and get into bed, they shot through the window, killing her. Unfortunately, the woman shot was the girlfriend's mother who had absolutely no relationship with the defendant.

I may have gotten a bit ahead of myself. The defendant in that case had shot and killed his seventeen-year-old victim after a brief argument at a Monday Night Football party. The shooting occurred on the second-floor steps of a three-story walkup apartment. The victim's cousin occupied the apartment, and two of his younger teenage cousins were eyewitnesses to the shooting. The victim was standing on a landing a few steps below the defendant. The single shot the defendant fired struck the victim in the right shoulder and travelled leftward and downward, piercing his heart.

The two teenage cousins gave sworn statements to the police, describing the shooting and the shooter. Other persons at the party told police that the defendant had been in attendance. The defendant was arrested the next day and had a handgun on his person; ballistics tests confirmed that it was the weapon used in the killing.

The two cousins were critical prosecution witnesses. As the trial date approached, both seemed to have disappeared from the face of the earth, and the hunt for them was on. The hunt lasted weeks, and my trial detective and I finally located them living in an apartment only two miles from where the shooting occurred.

Unsurprisingly, when we arrived at the apartment, one of the witnesses who was there was less than pleased to see us. We pushed our way through the door. The place was filthy. I still have a memory of an infant in diapers crawling on the floor of that cockroach infested dump. He said we could talk, and he ushered us into one of the bedrooms.

We thought the witness's actions to be odd, but we were not going to pass up the opportunity to speak with him. We later learned from one of the police officers in that municipality that he had been trying to gather enough information to establish probable cause for a search warrant at that apartment. He became aware through investigation that a cache of guns was kept there. That explains why the witness led us to another room.

After "motherfuckin" us ten or so times, we finally were able to explain to him that we were serving him with a Command to Appear subpoena, which meant that if he failed to appear for testimony, we would be back with a warrant for his arrest. He then defiantly told me that he did not recall anything from that night.

Just to clarify things, I asked if he was being truthful when he said he did not recall the events of that night. He said he was. I then asked if that was going to be his response to all questions I would ask during his trial testimony. He said it would be.

His defiance was the best thing that could have happened for the prosecution. When a witness feigns memory loss, the prosecution can request a hearing out of the jury's presence to establish that the previous sworn taped statement was made under circumstances establishing its reliability. If the judge determines it was, then the prior statement is admitted as evidence. At trial, the hearing was held, the judge determined the previous statement to be reliable, and I was allowed to play the statement as part of the witness's testimony.

Another witness who was dodging us in advance of trial was the female cousin who resided in the apartment where the victim was killed. Days before the trial was to start, we were outside her apartment viewing the scene. While there, I knocked on her door, and surprisingly, she answered. My detective and I then pushed our way into her apartment.

The apartment was small and there were three males sitting on a sofa across from where we entered. They were fidgeting, and "looked as nervous as three long-tailed cats in a room full of rocking chairs." I whispered to my detective to hand-serve the female with the Command to Appear subpoena we had brought. It was necessary to serve her with this type of subpoena, which was the first step in obtaining a Material Witness warrant should she not appear to testify.

When he sheepishly told me that he left it in the car, I told him to get it. He whispered to me, "But you don't have a gun." I whispered back that the occupants of the apartment didn't know that, and to get the subpoena. In the few minutes he was gone, the three males continued to fidget on the sofa. I kept reaching in the back belt line of my trousers as though I had a gun, and that kept the three males at bay.

We served the female with the subpoena, and my detective then asked the three males for identification. At that moment, one of the males jumped up from the sofa and bolted out the front door. We were later able to determine who he was, and that he had an open warrant for possession of a handgun.

The whole time we were preparing this case for trial and encountering witnesses who were very reluctant to testify, I thought the witnesses feared retaliation by the defendant. He had a substantial prior criminal record for crimes of violence and was a ranking member in the Crips. In other words, he was someone quite capable of doing them harm.

As I later discovered through other sources, these witnesses were hoping I would lose the trial so that they could murder the defendant, who would be released if acquitted. The jury's guilty verdict thwarted their plans. Witnesses seeking retribution are the most dangerous types of witnesses a prosecutor will encounter. Successfully prosecuting a defendant accused in a killing can often prevent another killing.

YOU SHOULDN'T HAVE SAID HE WAS MANIACAL

THERE CAN BE NO DOUBT that Brian Hoffman traveled from Florida to Somers Point, New Jersey, with a single purpose in mind. He was intent on murdering his ex-wife who had divorced him fifteen years before, and then he was going to kill their two daughters. To this end, he drove his green Ford F-150 truck bearing Florida tags up to New Jersey, and once he arrived, he began stalking his intended victims.

One of his daughters worked at a local bar, and one afternoon he followed her from her home as she was heading to her job. Realizing that she was being followed by a vehicle she did not recognize, she was eventually able to evade him. The incident left her shaken, and she discussed it with her mother, who told her to be careful because the person who was following her might be her father.

A day or two later, as her mother was out gardening in her yard on a beautiful fall weekday morning, Hoffman showed up again. The neighborhood in which the victim lived is very serene and made up of many nicely landscaped homes that border a fairway on one of the exclusive country clubs in the area. Hoffman pulled up in his truck, and with knife in hand, rushed his ex-wife and began stabbing her repeatedly.

Screaming for help, she tried fleeing to a neighbor's home. Hoffman grabbed hold of her in the neighbor's driveway, and while smashing her head against the bumper of the neighbor's car, he slit her throat. He told her that after he was done with her, he was going to kill their two daughters. The victim, who thought her life was over, was now only thinking of saving her daughters, and continued to scream for someone to help her stop this madman.

That morning, Mike Caiazza, who lived a block or so from the victim, heard those screams and jumped into action. Caiazza was a teacher and the wrestling coach at Egg Harbor Township High School, in a community adjacent to Somers Point. Upon hearing the victim's cry for help, Caiazza, who was home that morning because he was having arthroscopic knee surgery later that day, began climbing neighborhood fences, attempting to locate exactly where the screams were coming from.

When he scaled the last fence belonging to the victim's neighbor, he observed a horrible sight. Hoffman was slamming the victim's head into the concrete and continuing to stab her. Caiazza, a man small in stature but certainly not lacking in courage, shouted at Hoffman to "get the fuck off her," and in total disregard for his own safety, ran toward the danger to help the victim. At this point, Hoffman broke off the attack, ran to his truck, and sped away.

By now, one of the neighbors exited his home, and Caiazza shouted to "get some towels" so he could render first aid. The wounds Hoffman inflicted were deep, and he had "bisected" the victim's juggler vein. While police and emergency responders began arriving a short time later, it was the first aid that Caiazza rendered that saved her life. That is not just my opinion, but that of the trauma surgeon who testified at trial and whose skilled hands played a significant role in saving her.

As it was, she spent months in the hospital and a rehabilitation center receiving therapy to help recover from her serious injuries.

One of the first places Hoffman stopped as he tried to put as much distance between himself and local authorities searching for him was a shopping mall in King of Prussia, Pennsylvania, just outside Philadelphia. The investigation revealed that he stopped there and switched his Florida tags for Pennsylvania tags on a green Ford F-150 truck identical to his own. This way, any police officer running the tags would not be suspicious because the tags would come back to a green Ford F-150 truck.

I can say with certainty that Hoffman switched the tags because the owner of those tags testified they were stolen while he was shopping at the mall. Additionally, the Pennsylvania tags were on Hoffman's truck when he was found by a police officer from Signal Hill, California, who also testified at trial.

During the eighteen months Hoffman was on the lam, the case was aired on the national television show, *America's Most Wanted*, and law enforcement agencies across the country were participating in the search for him. He was constantly being tracked, and he managed to evade capture by law enforcement, who were at times just hours behind him. As he made his way west, Hoffman would stop at "labor ready" locations where he would work for a day to earn enough money to finance his flight. The fact that he had to provide a name and social security number to be paid allowed him to be tracked.

But what ultimately led to his arrest and capture in California was good old-fashioned police work. The night Hoffman was apprehended, an alert and astute Signal Hill Police Officer was on patrol in a residential area where several home and auto burglaries had occurred. When he saw Hoffman's truck with the Pennsylvania tags, he thought things looked out of place and decided to investigate further. He shined his flashlight in the bed of the truck, startling a sleeping Hoffman.

There were many unusual facts about this case, but the next one I will always remember. The officer asked Hoffman where he was from, and he responded, "New Jersey." He also asked Hoffman to provide identification, and once he did, the officer jokingly said, "If I run you, I'm not going to find that you're on *America's Most Wanted* or anything like that, am I?" To which Hoffman replied, "No, nothing like that." Ironically, *America's Most Wanted* had filmed a second episode about the case just weeks prior, and it was scheduled to air in a month or so.

When the officer ran him and found that Hoffman indeed had an open arrest warrant for an Attempted Murder charge in New Jersey, he immediately placed him under arrest and searched the truck, finding a knife. No, unfortunately forensic tests performed on the knife ruled it out as the knife used during the stabbing.

Hoffman was subsequently extradited to New Jersey where he defiantly demanded a trial to establish his innocence.

I was assigned the case, and fortunately for me and the citizens of New Jersey, the trial was assigned to Judge Albert Garofolo, the Presiding Criminal Judge for the Atlantic and Cape May County Vicinages. Neither a defendant nor a prosecutor could ask for a better trial judge than him. Before being appointed to the bench, Judge Garofolo tried cases both as a public defender and prosecutor. In fact, he was the first assistant prosecutor (second in command) who had interviewed me at the beginning of my career and was instrumental in me being hired as Assistant Atlantic County Prosecutor. His knowledge of substantive and procedural criminal law is second to none, his command of the rules of evidence is exceptional, and his pleasant, "laid back" demeanor and the respect he showed for everyone who appeared before him (he is now retired) made trying cases in his courtroom an absolute pleasure. Judge Garofolo is clearly in that subset of judges I previously described as being excellent.

I knew it was a blessing to have him as the trial judge from the moment I filed the initial pretrial motion. I sought to introduce a prior statement Hoffman made to a psychologist at the county jail to prove his state of mind regarding his motive and intent. He had been held many years prior for a domestic violence incident involving the victim, who at the time was his wife. Hoffman told the psychologist that once he was released, he "was going to kill his wife and that it would be worth it."

If you have watched enough episodes of the television show *Law and Order*, you might surmise that a statement made by a defendant to a treating psychologist would normally not be admissible at trial. It is protected by psychologist/patient privilege, and its admissibility against that person would discourage them from seeking needed help.

Judge Garofolo, in a well-reasoned opinion, allowed the statement to come in through the testimony of the psychologist as part of the prosecution's case. His decision (spoiler alert) was affirmed on appeal. Ironically, years later and without my collaboration, my daughter chose this issue as her thesis topic for her master's degree in social work.

Other witnesses who testified at the trial included the victim's daughter, the victim herself, therapists who treated the victim in her recovery, emergency medical personnel, detectives who processed the crime scene, and the arresting officer.

When the trial seemed like it could not have gotten more dramatic, Hoffman decided to testify in his own defense. Because of the volatility he demonstrated in committing the crime and our past experiences with similar defendants, the defense counsel, Judge Garofolo, and I all felt a little more on edge. I truly remember thinking to myself that if Hoffman came off the witness stand at me, I wouldn't be waiting for officers to intercede. At the risk of creating a mistrial, I was going to knock him into next week. It's not that I am such a tough guy, but Hoffman was small in stature, and without a knife in his hand, he was not that tough either.

When questioned by his attorney on direct examination, Hoffman told the jury that he just wanted to talk with the victim that morning, and in a rage, she attacked him with a gardening tool. He went on to say that he was able to disarm her and was only acting in self-defense.

There is an old adage that should guide any lawyer's cross-examination of a witness: "Don't ever ask a question you don't know the answer to." In cross-examining Hoffman, I took the risk, and it paid dividends. When I asked Hoffman whether he disposed of the knife somewhere along the Atlantic City Expressway on his immediate flight from the crime scene so that I would not be able to use it in this trial against him, he responded, "That's not the reason at all." Then I violated the cardinal rule of cross-examination. I asked, "What was your reason?" Hoffman's reply?

"It was getting blood all over my upholstery."

While other evidence made the case strong, that one casually cold response from Hoffman may have sealed the guilty verdict. The jury must have considered (as I asked them to) why Hoffman would flee all the way to California, attempting to cover his tracks and dispose of evidence, if he were justifiably acting in self-defense. They found his testimony preposterous but were hours in deliberation before finding him guilty. Two jurors were sympathetic to Hoffman, but finally decided to follow the judge's final instructions to base their verdict on the facts and evidence, free from any "bias, prejudice, or sympathy."

Hoffman remained defiant during sentencing. Judge Garofolo, after telling Hoffman that "he exuded evil," sentenced him to the maximum of twenty-three years. Hoffman had to serve seventeen years before being eligible for parole.

The story does not end there. Years after this occurred, Judge Garofolo (who I consider a friend, even more so since we both retired) contacted me about getting together for lunch. At lunch, he asked me if I remembered the Hoffman case—I assured him I did—and he told me the following story.

Some years into his sentence, Hoffman asked another inmate whether he knew someone on the "outside" who would be willing to kill Judge Garofolo for a price. The inmate reported this conversation to prison authorities, and the state police investigated it. The investigation included interviewing Hoffman, who not surprisingly denied the allegation. The investigators contacted Judge Garofolo, informed him of what occurred, told him the investigation was concluded, and suggested if he had not already done so, to legally obtain a handgun.

Another reason I remember the Hoffman case is in affirming his conviction on appeal, the appellate court admonished me for calling Hoffman "maniacal" during my closing argument.

During our lunch together, Judge Garofolo suggested I consider getting a handgun for my protection. In the thousands of cases I prosecuted, Hoffman was the only defendant I felt might truly seek retribution against me once he was paroled. As a prosecutor or a judge, it's not an irrational thought, but one you must put out of your mind to do your job effectively. Judge Garofolo told me during our lunch that it was not so much his own safety that concerned him, but more so the safety of his family. I agreed; we shared the same fear regarding our families, and as such, I was monitoring Hoffman through the State Bureau of Prisons Inmate Locator website.

I told the judge the reasons I didn't need a handgun: first, I wasn't the person who insulted Hoffman by telling him he "exuded evil;" and second, if Hoffman darkened my doorstep, I would want to smash his head with a baseball bat because it would be more personal. Judge Garofolo called me a "crazy son of a bitch;" we laughed and ordered another drink. Recently, Hoffman died in prison. The judge and I were not among the mourners. Is that maniacal?

I WILL NEVER WIN THE MISS AMERICA PAGEANT

WHEN I BEGAN WORKING AS an assistant prosecutor and relocated my family to the Atlantic City area, one of the first things I learned was how important the Miss America Pageant was to area residents. In fact, the pageant was only surpassed in importance by saltwater fishing and deer hunting. I knew little about any of those things and was not really interested in the last two. This subjected me to initial harassment by one detective who labeled me as another 201er (201 was then the area code for North Jersey). I was certainly aware of the pageant's existence because my mom and sisters watched it every year, but it was not until I attended my first Miss America Parade on the Atlantic City Boardwalk that I completely understood the excitement surrounding the week-long event. If you were expecting this chapter to contain some juicy story about the Miss America Pageant, you are going to be disappointed. I was simply setting the stage for what is to come.

A home invasion robbery occurs when a thug pushes his way into a home, uses or threatens to use force against the homeowner or someone present, and then steals property. If no one is home to be threatened, it is a burglary and not a robbery. Contrary to widespread belief, legally your home can never be "robbed." Only people can be robbed. The home invasion robberies I prosecuted in my career usually occurred in urban areas and involved a drug dealer being robbed of his money and/or drugs. The only home invasion I prosecuted in a rural part of the county involved an eighty-five-year-old victim who was involved in nothing illegal. It was also a memorable prosecution.

The victim in the case had hired the defendant to do some painting in the home. What the defendant would have learned on the job was that the victim lived alone, had some nice furnishings, and must not have been fond of banks, since there were substantial amounts of cash secluded throughout the home in cabinets and drawers. The defendant did not steal any of the victim's cash while he worked for him—he would have been the prime suspect should anything be missing because other than the owner, he was the only person allowed access to the home. Instead, the defendant waited several months before returning to steal cash.

The victim was asleep in his home on the night of the robbery. The defendant may have known the victim would be there because he physically cut the phone lines before breaking into the house. The victim was awakened by a noise outside, and when he opened his front door to investigate, the defendant burst in. A struggle ensued, and even though the

defendant was some fifty years younger, the victim was initially able to fight off his attacker. At some point, however, the
victim fell to the ground, striking his head on a ceramic vase
that shattered. Dazed, the victim got to his feet, but the defendant pushed him out the front door and down four stairs. The
victim face-planted on the cement sidewalk at the bottom of
the stairs, and as he lay there bleeding and semi-conscious,
the defendant grabbed several thousand dollars and fled.

As I previously said, this crime took place in a rural area.
Behind the victim's home, it was half a mile of forest to the
nearest road, and his closest neighbor lived several hundred
yards away. Despite being seriously injured, the elderly victim managed to crawl from his front yard to the neighbor's
house seeking help. Police and emergency medical personnel arrived shortly thereafter, and the victim was able to give
police a physical description of his assailant. There was a
flashlight found at the scene which the defendant must have
dropped while fleeing. It would have been especially useful
to the defendant as he was making his way through the dark
woods to the road behind the victim's house.

The flashlight would also have been useful in prosecuting
the defendant if the police had taken the time to examine
it for fingerprints. The description given by the victim was
transmitted to patrol officers, and about an hour later, one of
those officers saw the defendant exiting the woods. When the
officer approached him, the defendant tried unsuccessfully to
get away. He was found in possession of a large amount of
cash, arrested, and photographed.

The victim was taken to the hospital by ambulance and

remained there for several weeks, recovering from injuries that included a concussion. Detectives photographed the victim's battered and bruised face. Days later, police showed the victim a photographic lineup, and he recognized the defendant as his assailant. A conviction in the case was not guaranteed; I knew the defense would get some mileage out of arguing that the elderly victim was confused and picked the defendant's photo because he recognized him as his painter, not his assailant.

In preparing for trial, my assigned detective and I not only went to the victim's home to observe the scene, but we also had the arresting officer show us where he observed the defendant coming out of the woods. To determine exactly where it was in relation to the victim's home, we needed to view it from the air and take photographs. It just so happened my detective was going up in a state police helicopter the very next week to take other photographs, and I told him I would be coming along.

It was a windy and rainy morning when we hopped in the state police helicopter at the airport. On the drive over, my detective looked a bit squeamish about flying in that weather. To ease his angst, I told him that if we survived, I would treat him to lunch at our favorite Chinese buffet. We had arranged in advance for the patrol officer to stand exactly where he observed the defendant coming out of the woods on the night of the robbery, and from the sky we were able to observe that his position was directly in line with the victim's home. The blown-up photo we would use at trial was additional circumstantial evidence we could offer the jury to establish that the defendant was the perpetrator.

On the way back to the airport, the pilot was kind enough to fly over my house, much to the excitement of my wife and son who were in the backyard waving. When we finally touched down, we were so dizzy from the rough flight that the Chinese food I'd promised my detective had to wait an hour.

I caught a break at trial when the defendant did not appear after jury selection. A criminal defendant is not required to attend trial, but he must be present for the verdict. As the law requires, the judge told the jury that it was not to draw any negative inference from the defendant's absence, but his absence meant that now I could ask the victim to make an in-court identification of the defendant by showing him the same photo police used in the lineup.

The victim was the most important prosecution witness. I never showed him the photographs police took of his injuries during trial preparation because I wanted him to see them for the first time on the witness stand, for maximum emotional effect. It almost worked. While he proved to be an incredibly sympathetic witness, he had been so bruised and battered in the photos that he wasn't able to authenticate them as I had anticipated. Tears welled up in his eyes as he looked at the photos and said, "Oh my, is that really me? I would never win Miss America looking like this."

Since he could not say conclusively that the person in the photos was him (because he "couldn't look at himself in the mirror for weeks"), I needed to call the detective who took the photos to authenticate that they were photos of the victim taken in the hospital. Without proper authentication, the photos would not have gotten into evidence. I could tell the jury really liked and sympathized with the victim. The defense counsel, sensing no real value in victimizing him again in front of the jury, went soft in cross-examining him on his prior out-of-court identification of the defendant. A case that had looked difficult because of the victim's age ended well, with fewer pitfalls than anticipated.

The jury found the defendant guilty in less than an hour. After receiving the verdict, the judge told the jurors that the defendant was a fugitive and could be additionally charged with bail jumping. As the jurors were filing out, one of them said to me, "Find him." He was found the very next day at his residence and sentenced to a lengthy prison term.

For the next five years or so until he passed, the victim and I exchanged Christmas cards.

HAVE I GOT A CASE FOR YOU

WHEN THE CHIEF ASSISTANT PROSECUTOR in charge of the Investigations Section of the office came to me and said, "Have I got a case for you," I immediately thought there must be something wrong with the proofs. Normally, if a prosecutor from that section came to a prosecutor assigned to the Litigation Section, especially the Trial Section, it meant the case was a "dump job."

While we were all part of the same team, there was a bit of animosity between the two sections, with the Trial prosecutors looking upon Investigations as the "country club" of the office. As an assistant prosecutor, the county prosecutor had made his bones in Investigations, and he said on more than one occasion that "anyone can try cases." He may have been right, but not just anyone can try cases well. When he became the county prosecutor, most of the resources and salary money were dedicated to that side of the office. As a proud Trial grunt, and not one to shy away from a difficult case, I accepted the challenge posed by this supposed "dump job."

The case did not look easy, but it seemed winnable to me. It was an arson case, which by itself is one of the more difficult crimes to prove, but that wasn't the only obstacle to conviction. The crime took place in Atlantic City, and the two Atlantic City detectives who had investigated the case were, at the time, charged in a federal indictment with drug trafficking. This created problems in terms of their believability. The case also relied heavily upon co-defendant "snitches" who had been involved in the arson and were testifying for the prosecution in exchange for a reduced sentence. Their cooperation would be something the defense counsel could exploit by arguing to the jury that their testimony was "bought and paid for," and therefore not credible. And finally, the defendant was represented by the best criminal defense lawyer in South Jersey. Overcoming those obstacles is what made the case challenging for me, and a "dump job" for Investigations.

The facts of the case were not complex. The building sought to be destroyed was a vacant row house that the owner had insured. The defendant was a realtor and a friend of the owner. The motive behind the arson was the proceeds the owner would collect from the insurance company if the building were to become a total loss, in say, a fire. To that end, the owner approached the defendant, asking him if he knew someone who would burn the building for a price. The defendant said he could find someone, and approached one of the cooperating witnesses, who worked as a maintenance person in buildings the defendant owned. That person contacted a friend of his, who readily agreed to set fire to the building for $300.

As you can imagine, this was much less than the other co-conspirators would gain from the building's destruction. This person, who I will call "The Match," was told by his maintenance person friend (who I will refer to as "The Middleman") that he would find a twenty gallon can of gasoline on the building's second floor next to a mattress. He was instructed to soak the mattress, trail the gasoline to the rear door, and light it.

The Match followed the instructions to the letter, and when he lit the gasoline, witness testimony described the explosion blowing him one hundred and fifty feet out the back door.

The explosion was intense. A neighborhood resident who lived just across the street saw the blast and testified that he "thought it was the end of the world." The roof of the building was completely lifted from the structure, and debris the size of the average office desk was blown hundreds of feet in all directions.

An expert arson witness who testified for the prosecution at trial said that had these bumbling arsonists known what they were doing, they could have blown up an entire city block. He further testified that under the circumstances, a quarter cup of gasoline had the same properties as a stick of dynamite. To this day, I surmise that the defendant might have been hoping The Match did not survive the blast.

The building was a total loss, and The Match did not do much better. He was seriously burned, and part of his clothing had melted to his skin. The Match needed medical attention but could not go to a hospital for fear he would be connected to the explosion and fire. Instead, he went to a relative's home, where he must have experienced excruciating pain while soaking in a bathtub trying to separate his clothing from his flesh.

Because of the circumstances of the fire, the previously mentioned Atlantic City arson detectives became involved. They started their investigation by contacting the building's owner. They were unaware of any connection he had with the defendant and knew nothing about the involvement of The Middleman and The Match. As hot as the fire was, the trail was cold.

Arson investigators from the prosecutor's office also got involved, and months later, a $25,000 Crimestoppers Reward was offered for information leading to the arrest and conviction of persons involved in the arson. Unfortunately for The Match, his relatives turned him in for the reward money. He was arrested, and knowing that he faced up to twenty years, offered to cooperate in the investigation for a reduced sentence.

The Match knew nothing about the defendant because all his dealings were with The Middleman. The county prosecutor's arson investigators had him agree to wear a "wire" (a recording device) and speak with The Middleman to obtain more information on who was involved in the conspiracy to burn the building. He went to The Middleman under the auspices of needing more money for continuing medical and legal expenses. During this recorded conversation, The Middleman said he would speak to the person behind the conspiracy and attempt to get The Match more money.

The Middleman was then arrested, and facing the same serious prison time, he named the defendant as part of the conspiracy. He also agreed to wear a wire and speak with the defendant in return for a reduced sentence. What transpired during that recorded conversation were "F-bomb" laden admissions from the defendant in which he said The Match could "go fuck himself" since they had previously agreed on a price for his services. "It was a fucking contract," he said.

I had to try the case twice after the first trial ended in a hung jury. The tally as we came to learn was eleven to one to convict. In a criminal case, the verdict must be unanimous; all twelve jurors must agree. There were rumors that the one hold out knew the defendant and did not disclose that fact during jury selection. That could have improperly influenced the juror's vote, and I could have requested that the juror be excused for cause if it had been revealed.

Undaunted, I prepared for the retrial with a better understanding of what I could expect from the defense counsel. My colleagues who'd had the displeasure of previously trying cases with that lawyer had warned me about him, and he lived up to his reputation; he was thoroughly prepared, and a "bully" in the courtroom. I always felt that the best way to defend against a bully was to bloody his nose first. Although you may take some lumps yourself, the bully will be reeling much longer. That was my strategy for round two.

Defense counsel seemed to appeal more to female jurors. In the retrial, I decided to go against the grain and put as many older women as I could on the jury. Hubris may have gotten the best of him, as he seemed to fail to consider how they might react to his client using "fuck" every other word in the recorded conversation I would be playing for them. They cringed every time they heard it.

Additionally, during the first trial, he'd used every objection he made as an opportunity to improperly present another summation to the jury. I asked the judge during the second trial to hear all objections at sidebar to prevent him from gratuitously making statements to the jury. My request was granted, which pissed defense counsel off to no end.

When The Match had testified at the first trial, he allowed defense counsel to beat him up a bit about being a cooperating witness who got a deal. In prepping him for the second trial, I told him to simply admit he got a deal because that was the truth. This time, when defense counsel started asking him about his deal, he responded, "Counselor, do you want me to tell the jury I got a deal?" Counsel then smugly told him, "If you got a deal, tell them you got a deal." The Match turned, faced the jurors, and looking them square in the eyes, said, "Jury, I gots a deal!" I got the feeling that the jury felt sorry for him. Particularly since, during my questioning, he had told them how the burns he suffered from were not worth the $300 he received for starting the fire.

Finally, I also decided to go more on the offensive in the retrial to rile defense counsel as much as possible. This might have been the most effective part of my trial strategy.

One peculiar thing about defense counsel was that he refused to represent anyone who was a "rat" (agreed to cooperate with the prosecution in return for a reduced sentence). In fact, he represented many alleged Philadelphia and Atlantic City organized criminals, and the code of silence was just as important to him as it was to them. As you now know, important to this prosecution were the two cooperating "rat" witnesses who had worn wires.

My wife (who I previously told you was the biggest supporter of my career as a prosecutor) took a peculiar interest in the case, probably because every night I came home from the first trial looking like four people had jumped me in an alley. She only attended closing arguments because after the first trial, she was familiar with the facts of the case and wanted to see how good defense counsel was during closing arguments. When defense counsel had finished excoriating the two "rat" witnesses for three hours, she said to me, "You're in trouble." I thanked her for boosting my confidence and went right after defense counsel's closing.

I started by saying, "Members of the jury, law enforcement has been trading time for the truth for many, many years. The reason it works is because persons involved in criminal conspiracies know they can help themselves by cooperating with prosecutors and giving truthful testimony."

While we were finishing this case, the John Gotti trial—the one that finally sent him to prison—was continuing in New York. I reminded the jury about that case, telling them that the government was only able to prosecute Gotti because a co-conspirator had become a cooperating witness. I looked at defense counsel, referred to that witness as the biggest "rat" of all time, and called him by name. Defense counsel went ballistic. The witness in the Gotti case was a local mobster he represented, and he spent at least the next ten minutes telling the court that that witness was not on trial here, and I had no business besmirching that person's character. The judge properly sustained his objection and told the jury to disregard my comments about the Gotti case.

The damage had already been done. I wonder if counsel later realized that he should have calmly raised his objection at sidebar. In vociferously defending his former client in the jury's presence, he was effectively criticizing himself for attacking the prosecution's two "rat" witnesses. The defendant was found guilty, and while his conviction was affirmed on appeal, the appellate court chastised me for my comments about the cooperating witness at the Gotti trial.

What could have borne upon the appellate court's decision to affirm was a letter the defendant wrote to the judge from jail between the time the jury rendered its verdict and sentencing. In that letter, he told the judge he'd been lying when he testified at trial that he had no part in the conspiracy.

It is unbelievably bad to tell a sentencing judge that in addition to being an arsonist, you are also a perjurer. The judge "threw the book" at him, sentencing him to a term of twenty-four years. It had been a long two years since my colleague came to me saying, "Have I got a case for you." By the way, the building's owner fled the country before he could be arrested, and to my knowledge, remains a fugitive.

THIRTY YEARS IS A LONG TIME

SHORTLY BEFORE I RETIRED, MY immediate boss asked me to evaluate a thirty-year-old homicide case to see if it was still provable. The U.S. Marshals Service had arrested the defendant in New York, and needed an answer as to whether our office would move to extradite him (ask the federal court there to order him returned to New Jersey) for a resolution of the charges.

The first place to start evaluating your chances in cases like this is to determine how many of your important witnesses are still alive. Knowing that I championed hopeless causes, he gave me his usual "you're an asshole" look when I told him that at least one witness (the deceased victim) was still unavailable to testify. The most exciting thing about the case for me was that trial preparation would be a reunion of sorts with several detectives who had long since retired. If I determined that the defendant should be extradited, I was almost guaranteeing that it would be assigned to me.

Thirty years earlier, the defendant in the case had been involved in the wholesale business of selling marijuana in Atlantic City. The intended victim was one of his retailers, and when he ended up owing the defendant several hundred dollars, the defendant came gunning for him. It might seem unreasonable to the reader that anyone would kill someone over several hundred dollars. Not necessarily. I once tried a defendant who fatally shot his victim over five dollars' worth of marijuana.

These facts were not complex. The retailer was seated in the passenger's seat of a parked car owned by his friend, who was seated in the driver's seat when the shooting occurred. The defendant approached the passenger's side and fired six shots pointblank at the passenger. He was struck with five of the six and survived. The driver was not as fortunate. One bullet struck him and passed completely through his body, puncturing his heart and killing him.

The most crucial witness in the case was the passenger. He could identify the defendant as the shooter because he had worked for him selling marijuana. The lead detective in the case and most of the police witnesses were former MCS detectives. They were all still available to testify at trial. Other witnesses in the case who could corroborate parts of the evidence essential to proving the defendant's guilt were either missing or deceased.

Besides the missing and dead witnesses, the case was difficult for several reasons. Normally, a prosecutor would shy away from trying a case in which only a single witness can identify the shooter, especially when that witness is a drug

dealer who was susceptible to being robbed at gunpoint by
anyone who knew him. Customarily, drug dealers are in possession of drugs and money, the proceeds of sale. That fact
did not concern me much because of the surviving victim's
relationship with the defendant, and the defendant's strong
motive for shooting the retailer who owed him money.

The second obstacle was that the evidence connecting the
defendant to his apartment, where a large quantity of marijuana was found, and to a vehicle he used in fleeing the area,
containing evidence tying him to both, would be rightfully
excluded.

The trial judge eventually ruled that the warrant obtained
to search the apartment was invalid. A search warrant must
"particularly" describe the place to be searched, and this warrant did not. The suppressed evidence was important in proving the defendant's motive.

Additionally, the passage of time certainly benefited the
defendant because witness memories fade along with it. It
particularly benefited him since, based upon my review, he
would not be calling any witnesses in his defense, while his
lawyer would have the opportunity to challenge the memory
of each prosecution witness.

Finally, this defendant enjoyed the advantage of being
prosecuted under the law as it had existed thirty years prior.
This meant that, if convicted, he would serve approximately
one third of any sentence he received for the killing, instead
of eighty-five percent as current New Jersey law required. I
decided that he should not be allowed to get away with murder. Casting fate to the wind, I recommended that he be

extradited so the case could finally move forward. My prediction was right. The case was assigned to me.

Humorous things happened over the course of this prosecution, and it began with trial preparation. As I typically do when preparing police witnesses, I brought all the detectives that had been involved in the investigation together at the same time. This helps them recall details as they listen to each other describe their roles in the investigation and establishes consistency in their trial testimony. It almost worked.

One of the detectives insisted that a photo lineup had been shown to the victim while he was in the hospital recovering from his wounds, and he positively identified the defendant as the person who shot him. This would have been substantial evidence, since the closer in time to the incident that a witness makes an out-of-court identification, the more reliable the in-court identification of the defendant becomes. In fact, the judge tells the jury that they can infer this in their deliberations when determining the facts of the case.

The lineup would certainly have been documented somewhere in the case file, but it was not, because it never happened. I had my trial detective document and forward this newly discovered evidence to defense counsel, but instead of strengthening the prosecution's case, it made it appear as though the detective had added a false detail to bolster a thirty-year-old case. Though it did bring about a funny exchange between the group of detectives.

"What the fuck are you talking about? That never happened," they told him.

"I have to take medicine for my memory," he replied.

To which another detective quipped, "Well, you better fucking take it for clarity on the day you testify."

Another humorous fact had been revealed during trial prep shortly after they arrived on scene the day of the homicide. Information about the defendant's involvement in the shooting and his residence in a second-story walk-up apartment nearby was discovered in the first hour. Four MCS detectives went to the apartment and cautiously began climbing the stairs. Before reaching the top, they collectively realized that none of them were armed. They had all left their service weapons back at the office. Fortunately, they were able to borrow the revolver of a uniformed Atlantic City police officer who escorted them to the apartment. The defendant was obviously not there.

The laughs just kept coming at trial. As you know from previous chapters, I am technologically deficient. I had some ideas in terms of visual aids for trial, but without the help of one of the agents in the office, they would have never come to fruition. She was a wiz when it came to PowerPoint presentations; I told her what I envisioned, and she made it happen. The street where the shooting had taken place thirty years before was a one-way, single-lane street that ran to the Boardwalk. That same street was widened to two lanes, most of the houses were torn down, and one of the largest casinos in Atlantic City was now at the end of the street abutting the Boardwalk. I wanted to show it then and now, because I wanted the jury to see there was little chance of escape for the victims after the defendant started shooting.

Crime scene photos taken thirty years ago were blended

so that those photos faded into how the street appeared now. The agent was not happy when I told her that I needed her to operate the equipment during the trial because, if left alone, I would surely botch the presentation. She was much more nervous than I as the opening statements approached. We had rehearsed the opening to ensure the presentation would flow. Things were going great until I said, "Here's what the street looked like then and now," which was her cue to show the "now." Instead of fading, the screen went completely white. I glanced at the agent, who appeared on the verge of fainting as she nervously fidgeted with the equipment.

Without missing a beat, I told the jurors that that is what the street would be like in a blizzard. The jury had a good laugh; snowfalls are rare for Atlantic City winters. The delay caused by the malfunction lasted less than a minute, and when the Court recessed after both opening arguments, the agent was very apologetic. I thanked her for the miscue and assured her that it's not often a prosecutor can inject a little levity into a homicide case. We had scored more jury points with the mistake than we would've with a perfect execution. It made us look human in the jury's mind, and our presentation more natural than rehearsed.

The defense attorney in the case did an excellent job representing his client in the pre-trial phase. He was successful not only with his motion to suppress physical evidence, but also with a motion to exclude a statement the defendant made at the time of his arrest. That statement would have bolstered the prosecution's case regarding the defendant's consciousness of guilt. It was time now to see how skilled he was at trial.

The MCS detective who had led the investigation was one of the first prosecution witnesses. I was impressed with defense counsel's cross-examination. He hammered away at things this detective did not do and duties he did not fulfill. There is an adage shared and often used by criminal lawyers on both sides. "If the facts are against you, pound the law with the jury, and if the law is against you, pound the facts. If both the facts and the law are against you, pound the table." Defense counsel's pounding of the table during his cross-examination was effective because it did not appear as though he was personally attacking the witness.

He built to a crescendo, and then undid all that he had accomplished by committing the cardinal sin of cross-examination. He asked a question when he did not know the answer. It went like this.

Defense counsel: "Detective, you would agree with me would you not, that there were a number of things you failed to do as part of your investigation?"

Witness: "Yes. I would agree."

Defense counsel (sarcastically): "Was this your very first homicide investigation?"

Witness (sheepishly): "Yes, it was."

The jury collectively smiled and had no doubt believing that everything he testified to was the truth. With that single honest answer, the jury saw him as one of themselves—human.

When you self-inflict a wound like defense counsel had just done, it is important as a trial attorney to give the jury a look like you were expecting the answer. A trial attorney should never end cross-examination at a point where the witness has the edge; minimize the damage by returning to questions that exposed the witness's vulnerability. I know this as a trial attorney who has on occasion wounded myself. Defense counsel did neither and exposed his own vulnerability.

The next day, I decided to test counsel's vulnerability. While the prosecution was going well, the entire case would still come down to the believability of the victim's testimony. I previously mentioned that the defendant's car was located close to the crime scene. The car was loaded with clutter, and I mean loaded. There were clothes, cigarette butts, old mail, old receipts, small change—a plethora of crap. Everything in that car, except for the old mail, was useless to me. The old mail was important in proving that the address where the marijuana was found was the defendant's residence.

My problem, however, was that I did not have the marijuana as evidence in the case because it had been suppressed (excluded) by the judge. Without the marijuana, the jury would need to fully believe the victim's testimony that he had sold marijuana for the defendant, owed him money he could not pay, and that this was why the defendant shot him.

My plan was to throw defense counsel off his game, and to do that, I needed to persuade defense counsel that something in the car was very damning to the defendant.

Again, because the marijuana was suppressed, there was minimum probative value to the crap in the car. The second person I had to convince was the judge. Under the Rules of Evidence, either side can, when appropriate, ask a judge to hold a hearing out of the jury's presence to determine whether certain evidence is admissible during trial. I asked, and the judge granted my request for the hearing. It remained to be seen whether the "when appropriate" requirement would come back to bite me on the ass.

The witness who testified at the hearing was the former captain of MCS detectives. As part of the investigation, he'd inventoried every item found in the car. Before he took the stand, I told him I was going to question him about every item found in the car. He said, "Everything? That will take hours, and much of this shit won't help your case at all." He was right, and I asked him to trust me on this one.

After the first hour or so of listening to, "McDonald's wrapper, toothpick, used Kleenex ..." the judge had heard enough. He told me to submit the list of items, along with the statements of any witnesses who could corroborate the fact that the defendant resided at the address where the marijuana was found. He did make it clear, and rightfully so, that no testimony was coming in about the marijuana itself.

I attached the statements of the corroborating witnesses to the inventory and sent it into the judge. The captain seemed to know the case better than defense counsel because during the recess, he asked if I was crazy, pointing out that some of those witnesses had not yet been found, and maybe never would be.

The judge gave us his ruling over an hour later. The stuff in the car tying the defendant to the residence could be admitted, but only through the testimony of the witnesses submitted for his review.

Now I was really in deep shit, because when it came time and I failed to produce those witnesses, the judge would be really pissed that three hours of his time had been wasted on evidence that still wasn't coming into the trial.

Thinking quick, I said to defense counsel, "That ruling was some kick in the balls for your client." He looked defeated and asked whether I would consider allowing his client to plead guilty to the initial plea offer. I told him no way since we were far along, and a great amount of time and resources were spent in preparing for trial. He made a counteroffer, which I declined, but told him what offer I would accept. That last offer was a little less than what the defendant would receive if the trial continued, and he was found guilty. A big "if" indeed.

The captain was watching the entire negotiations and said it took a "brass set of balls" to hold out for the last plea offer. Especially because, had the defendant refused to accept and we continued with a trial, the judge would now be pissed at the prosecution.

An hour later, the defendant entered a guilty plea. The calculated bluff paid off. It was a long time coming, but after thirty years, justice was finally served.

BUSTING A GUT

I WAS JUST NOT FEELING right as I headed for work on that steamy July morning. There was a stabbing pain in my left side, which I attributed to a muscle I might have pulled while painting our house over the weekend. I was scolding myself for not having climbed down and moved the ladder instead of reaching as far out as I could to cover that last spot on the wall. At the same time, I was convincing myself that the pain would dissipate as the day wore on, hopefully in time to see the local minor league baseball team that night with our kids. It was "Fireworks Night," and we were excited about attending.

By the end of the day, as I continued to feel worse, I went to my supervisor to see if she would excuse me from a mandatory meeting that afternoon. My reputation having preceded me, she said that while I would do anything to avoid these meetings (and she was right about that), using illness as an excuse was a first for me. She said that the meeting would be kept short and that she expected to see me there. I went back to my desk to finish a legal brief I was working on. Not long after, I passed out.

When I awoke, I thought I was having a strange nightmare. The detective assigned to me at the time, Nick Erman, is a big man with a booming voice. I was in an unmarked car and Nick was driving—fast. We didn't have the usual flashing lights or siren because, as you previously read, the county prosecutor minimized the importance of the Trial Section and assigned some of the worst fleet vehicles to it. Instead, he was shouting over the car's radio, which doubled as a loudspeaker, for other drivers to "get the fuck out of the way." We arrived at one of the local hospitals—which would not have been my first choice—and I was whisked into the emergency room. It would be the beginning of a three-day odyssey.

As I began to reorient myself, Nick explained to me that he walked into my office and, finding me unconscious and non-responsive, threw me over his shoulder, placed me in the car, and proceeded "pedal to the medal" to the hospital. Nick and I were paired together for about two years. He was an outstanding municipal police officer before being hired by the prosecutor's office. Nick's "street smarts" and good instincts made him an excellent trial investigator. We had a lot of fun working together, and not only were we a successful trial team, but we also became as close as brothers during those two years.

The emergency room was packed with people waiting to be treated, and it looked like I was going to be there awhile. To make matters worse, the hospital's nursing staff was participating in a job action, slowing things down even more than usual. I called my wife to tell her I was at the hospital and might be delayed. She assumed I was there speaking to a prospective witness—a reasonable assumption, since nine times out of ten, I would have been there for that reason—and told me to "wrap it up" and get home because we were going to the ballgame that night. I finally convinced her that I was not joking and was there seeking medical attention.

It was about two hours after I arrived that someone made the decision to X-ray my abdomen to diagnose the problem. When I was shown that X-ray, I said to Nick, "It's true what people say about lawyers, Nick. They don't have a heart." That brought a laugh from the crowd of people who were back with us in triage. I thanked Nick again for taking me to the hospital and tried to convince him to go home as it was getting well into the evening. He said he was not leaving until he knew I would be okay.

Another hour passed before I met with a physician, and I became a bit more concerned when he told me he was a gastroenterology surgeon. He said that he did not believe my problem was appendicitis but was waiting for my lab work to totally rule it out. He also said that I was being admitted to the hospital for treatment, and that whether it was my appendix or not, he was going to remove it at midnight. I asked him if he could do the surgery laparoscopically—we were beginning our annual family Maine camping trip in just a few days—he said no, and headed out before I could ask another question. I finally convinced Nick to leave telling him, "I'll see you tomorrow—maybe."

I'd never had surgery before, and as the hours slowly

approached midnight, my level of concern increased. Midnight came and went, and no one said a thing or could provide me with any answers. I had not eaten all day and was not allowed to eat anything while awaiting surgery. I was unable to sleep all night, ruminating over what the surgeon had told me. I was thinking crazy thoughts like, *if he removed a healthy appendix would it be cosmetic surgery and would my health insurer deny coverage making me responsible for the bill?*

Night turned into dawn, dawn turned into day, and by 10 a.m., I had worked myself up to a feverish pitch. Doubled over and in pain, I made my way to the nurses' station across from my room, demanding to see the chief surgeon, the medical claims person, the patient liaison, and to be given a phone book. I remember a young intern being there who I had heard giggling with the nurses, and when he stood up to heroically defend them against this screaming maniac (me), I told him to "sit the fuck down because I'm not feeling that weak." He sat back down. Why the phone book? I was looking for a second opinion, and additionally, wanted to call the office of the surgeon I spoke with the previous night.

While I was able to speak with his office, the receptionist told me he was not in and had no idea where he was. About thirty minutes later, I received a call from the first assistant prosecutor. He asked me what was going on, and I told him I had no idea, that the surgeon was either going to remove my tonsils or my testicles, but he could not be found. I was being generous in thinking he called to ask how I was feeling. I learned days later that the hospital called him attempting to control me. About thirty minutes after his call, the surgeon entered my room in his scrubs, having just come from surgery. Lacking any bedside manner, he said, "What's your problem?" I told him that he was my problem and reminded him of what he told me the night before. "Do you think because you are a lawyer—" I interrupted him before he could finish the sentence by telling him I would have gone to medical school, but my father could not afford the golf lessons. He told me I was now on the surgical schedule for 3 p.m. before storming out of my room.

The next visit I got was from the surgeon's father, who was also a surgeon. He was old school in that he could not have been nicer or more kind. His bedside manner was completely opposite that of his son. He said his son had consulted him about my case the night before and he explained that while it was not appendicitis, if abdominal surgery became necessary, a surgeon would remove a healthy appendix since an appendectomy becomes riskier as we grow older. He explained that everyone has small fatty deposits on their intestines and that through rigorous activity, these deposits can sometimes twist and ulcerate.

When I asked about my options, particularly if I could go home, he said going home would require me to check in with him every ten minutes because the ulcerated deposits could burst, resulting in life-threatening peritonitis. That was not a feasible option. He said the second option was exploratory surgery to fully diagnose the problem and repair any damage. I asked him how long the surgery would normally take, and he said one to two hours.

He was a real gentleman, and while we talked, he told me

he had been trying unsuccessfully to get information about a case that was pending in my office. Since there was nothing untoward about the information he was seeking, I made a phone call and was able to get an immediate answer to his question. I asked him if it were possible for him to do the surgery laparoscopically; he said that he would, and that he would speak to his son about performing it that way. Not a bad quid pro quo.

My wife called shortly thereafter, and I briefed her on my conversation with the surgeon's father, telling her surgery was scheduled for 3 o'clock. She said she and our children would be by at noon to see me. They arrived promptly at noon and were there for only a few minutes before an orderly came in with a gurney telling me I was next. I gave my kids and wife a quick hug, told them that I loved them, and off we went.

While I was being prepped for surgery, nurses and the anesthesiologist were introducing themselves as they administered an injection. My reaction to the injection was immediate and allergic. The last things I remembered were a feeling like something hot was shooting through my body, vomiting, and the anesthesiologist telling me to "make sure to get this on your record when you are out of surgery." The surgery lasted some six hours. The deposits had ulcerated and burst, leaving me with a gut full of toxic fluid that had to be removed.

As you may recall, I'd never had surgery or general anesthesia before. When I came to in post-op, it was as though I had awoken from a nightmare. I was attached to all kinds of tubes, had tremendous pain in my gut, and was totally disoriented. My first thought was that I had been shot, and I started pulling out tubes because I was going to find the bastard who shot me. I must have been out of control because my wife was brought in to restore order. She promptly did.

I eventually got back to my room, still in pain and wearing leg pads that looked like hockey goalie pads. The next day when I was being discharged, my wife asked me how long those pads had been on without being connected to a machine. The pads prevent your blood from clotting—if they are attached to a machine. They never were.

The nurse who met me in my room told me not to get out of bed and to use the buzzer if I needed anything. Hours later, I needed something. I had to urinate, but the urinal was full, so I started pushing the buzzer. After about ten minutes, no one was responding, even though I could hear the nurses talking at the station across from me. I stood up, and feeling now like I had been stabbed, fell back into bed. Undaunted, I grabbed the IV stand attached to me, pulled myself up, and banged off the walls as I made it to the toilet in my room.

The commotion must have been loud because the nurse came in and started bitching at me for not using the buzzer and getting out of bed. When I told her I tried, she essentially called me a liar, saying she was out there the whole time and did not hear any buzzer. She finally realized I was telling the truth when she kept pushing the buzzer and no one responded. I did not expect an apology from her and could not refrain from telling her, "I guess it was a good thing that I was not in cardiac arrest." She left in a huff.

I was discharged the next day and grateful to be home. I guess you could say I busted a gut to get into the hospital and busted a gut to get out. We were able to travel to Maine the next week and had a wonderful vacation.

TRYING TIMES THREE

WHEN A JURY IS UNABLE to reach a unanimous verdict, what is referred to as a "hung jury" occurs. The judge declares a mistrial and then it is incumbent upon the prosecutor to determine whether to: dismiss the charges against the defendant; offer the defendant a more lenient sentence in return for a guilty plea; or retry the case with another jury. Few prosecutors enjoy trying the same case a second time. In a retrial, it is difficult to muster the same enthusiasm generated by the adrenaline rush of attempting to convince a group of twelve strangers to accept a position based on facts the prosecution anticipates will be persuasively presented through witnesses.

Another reason that bodes against trying a case again is that prosecution witnesses are locked into testimony given at the first trial, and any deviation subjects them to greater juror scrutiny; defense counsel always uses transcripts of prior testimony to challenge the witness's veracity and memory. Finally, a retrial is usually the last chance for conviction. While no set number of times exists for retrying a defendant, appellate courts normally frown upon a third prosecution unless circumstances have changed. A retrial is bad enough. Trying a case for a third time is masochistic.

Two of the three defendants I was prosecuting in this shooting case were being tried for a third time. The changed circumstance allowing for the second retrial was that the third defendant involved in the shooting was a fugitive for the first two trials. The first two attempts were near misses. In fact, there was a lone holdout juror that prevented a conviction in the first retrial. Therefore, the likelihood of conviction was good in a second retrial.

Another factor weighing in favor of a second retrial was that these defendants had a reputation for violence in the community where the crime occurred, and they were confident that witnesses would not testify in a third trial for fear of retaliation. For that reason, they were unwilling to accept any plea offer which required prison time. Finally, the most important reason the case cried out for a second retrial was the severity of the crimes.

As you now know, the case involved a shooting. The defendants drove into the courtyard of a public housing complex in a dark-colored SUV. It was one of the first warm days of spring, and the courtyard was crowded with young children and other residents enjoying the weather. The defendants circled the parking lot that abutted the courtyard, located their intended victim, and parked. One of defendants then jumped from the vehicle and opened fire with a TEC-9, a semi-automatic weapon with a magazine that holds thirty rounds of ammunition.

All thirty rounds were fired because thirty shell casings were recovered as part of the investigation. The intended victim managed to flee the area without being shot, and miraculously, the children and all residents escaped being shot. Unfortunately, a man who was there visiting a friend was not as lucky. One of the bullets struck him in the chest, seriously wounding him. The defendants fled the scene in the SUV, but not before one of the persons in the courtyard was able to get a partial tag number.

Police arrived at the location within minutes of the shooting and called for an ambulance to rush the wounded victim to the hospital. They also secured the crime scene to preserve evidence, and interviewed the witness who gave them the vehicle description and partial tag number. Police searched the surrounding area, but the defendants were not immediately found. They did, however, have an idea who was involved, and later that day stopped the vehicle in a neighborhood near where the shooting occurred. The partial tag number given matched the first three numbers on the SUV's tags. The TEC-9 was not in the vehicle, and the vehicle was not registered to any of the three defendants.

You may be asking yourself why this case was tried three times given this evidence. The fact that the three defendants were found in a vehicle matching the description and partial tag number the witness provided was circumstantial evidence that they were involved in the shooting. The intended victim was never identified, and as such, never came forward with any information about the shooting. None of the other people in the courtyard provided any useful information to the police, which was not unusual given the violent nature of what they just witnessed and their fear of retaliation.

Evidence justifying their fear was expressed by the wounded victim, who recovered after spending several weeks in the hospital. When I spoke with him in preparation for the first trial, he asked if I could try the case without him. I told him it would be difficult and since he did not see the shooter or the SUV, he would only be asked to testify about his being present at the scene, being shot, and the nature of his wounds. He really hoped to avoid testifying, telling me that he survived a combat tour in Vietnam and did not want to be gunned down in the streets of his hometown.

He did eventually testify at all three trials. The witness who gave police the vehicle description and partial tag was an alcoholic. She lived in the neighborhood where the shooting occurred and was absolutely petrified about testifying at trial. The poor woman was shaking during her testimony, was not particularly articulate, and the three defense attorneys beat her up on the stand about her drinking and what she had "actually" seen that day. During their closing arguments (as was their duty to their client), they attacked her believability regarding whether the tag number she gave to the police was accurate. They argued that since the gun was never recovered, there was not sufficient evidence presented by the prosecution tying their clients to the shooting.

The evidence at the second retrial, or third trial as it were, was the same with one exception. The woman who testified about the partial tag did not appear and could not be found. Normally, the prosecution would be S.O.L. (shit out of luck).

Because the witness was hand-served with a Command to Appear subpoena, exhaustive efforts were taken by the prosecution to locate her, and since defense counsel had cross-examined her at the first two trials, her previous testimony was allowed to be read into the record by the court reporter.

As you may recall from a previous chapter, that testimony is read in a monotone voice and loses the impact that a jury would get from viewing the witness's body language. The icing on the cake at the second retrial was that the defendant, who possessed but was not the owner of the SUV, was brazen enough to drive it to the trial and park it in front of the courthouse. At my direction, my assigned detective photographed the defendant getting in and out of the SUV. He then testified about these photographs. As I stated previously, it is sometimes better to be lucky. The defendants were convicted, sentenced to a substantial prison term, and the conviction was upheld on appeal.

In between the initial trial and first retrial, the defendants were charged in another shooting. This time one of the stray bullets they fired struck a nine-year-old child playing in his yard. Fortunately, the child only suffered a graze wound. Evidence of that shooting could not be introduced at either the first or second retrial because it may have "prejudiced" the jurors.

A year or so after the second retrial concluded, I was at a self-wash washing my car. A woman waiting behind me approached and asked me if I recognized her. I told her I did. She then confirmed for me that she was the holdout juror from the first retrial. I then told her, as is required, that I was not permitted to speak with her about the case unless she would be willing to testify under oath in open court, if called upon to do so, about whatever she told me.

She acknowledged she would, and I then asked her if she learned after the trial that the defendants were involved in another shooting during which a child was wounded. She said she was, and that that "didn't matter" to her. She said she wanted to tell me why she could not vote to convict. I wanted to tell her that her reason really didn't matter to me, but instead I politely asked her if it would "matter" if it was her own child who was wounded. Her silence confirmed that our conversation was over. I wished her well, got in my car and drove away.

DINING OUT ON THE JOB

I LIKED WORKING WITH DETECTIVES who enjoyed a good meal. If you happened to be out on the hunt or were scheduled to interview a witness for a trial and were in the vicinity of a good eatery, it made no sense to not include lunch as part of the day. In fact, there reached a point in my career when some detectives volunteered for a "road trip" with me because they knew it might involve fine dining. Often it was a detective who was introducing me to a new favorite place.

Bruce DeShields is a bear of a man who, at first glance, cuts an imposing figure. It does not take long to find out that he is one of the nicest, most decent, and kind people you will ever know. He is gregarious, has a terrific sense of humor, and an ability "to talk the fruit off the trees." This last quality made him an extremely effective interviewer. Bruce could become your minister, priest, rabbi, or total confidant. This ability allowed him to take many confessions from accused murderers. He worked in every unit in the office and retired as chief of county detectives.

Not only is he a great cook, but Bruce, like me, enjoys tasty food, with ambiance not being a deal-breaking factor. He and I were out one day to view a crime scene in a neighboring county, and Bruce suggested we stop out for "the best barbeque chicken sandwich in the world."

We stopped at a roadside stand next to a tavern attended by an elderly African American gentleman. We ordered two chicken sandwiches, and he said it might be a while because he was by himself. It was no problem for us because it was a beautiful spring day and there were tables outside; I went next door and picked up a six-pack to help us pass the time.

After an hour we were down to our last two beers. I was ready to purchase another six-pack when we were told our order was ready. When the proprietor gave us our sandwiches he was staring over our shoulders as if there was a long line of customers behind us, the only two people there. We paid and thanked him, to which he replied, "I've got to get me some help." Bruce was right about the chicken sandwiches. We thoroughly enjoyed them and the elderly proprietor's comment.

Kevin Ruga was another excellent detective assigned to me. He worked for a small but busy police department before coming to the prosecutor's office. Kevin is a quiet person. He is bright, has great instincts, and relates to people very well. He and I once had to interview police witnesses at the department he'd left, and I joked with the chief that Kevin was the most unique police officer I'd ever seen: he does not drink, and I have never heard him utter so much as a curse word.

One of my favorite experiences with Kevin occurred

while we were interviewing a security guard at a pharmacy in Atlantic City. The case involved a serial shoplifter who became a robber when he started beating on a store clerk who tried to stop him from stealing merchandise. While talking with the security guard in his office at the rear of the store, we noticed that one of the walls in the office was full of photographs of people who had shoplifted at that location, been caught, and then excluded from the store. The guard explained to me that not every shoplifter was prosecuted since that would require him to spend more time in court than in the store.

As a prosecutor, you must have a detective with you when interviewing a witness to avoid becoming a witness yourself, since the person you are speaking with might provide new or additional information. That information must be turned over to the defense. The office had a security camera that scanned the premises, and while I was conducting the interview, Kevin was listening and watching the camera. I had to stop the interview when Kevin abruptly left the office. He'd seen a shoplifter and nabbed him during the interview. How's that for multi-tasking?

My second favorite experience with Kevin was a meal we shared at a luncheonette in an adjoining county. We had been to that county jail to speak with a witness, and surprisingly, we finished right around lunchtime. Also, we were just down the street from the luncheonette that I was very anxious to go to. The Angel's Mike Trout, a hometown guy, often eats there in the off-season. Kevin had been there many times and suggested we go to try out the house specialty, a hamburger served with the owner's special sauce.

It was delicious! The sauce was much like one I'd enjoyed as a child at a Texas red hots place near where my wonderful grandma lived in Buffalo, New York. Thank you, Kevin! It was not just a meal; it was a memory.

Newark New Jersey's Iron Bound section has some fine Portuguese restaurants that I'd discovered while attending law school and working in Newark. Many serve a garlic shrimp dish that is mouthwatering, and their paella is outstanding. One favorite restaurant of mine serves homemade soup, a salad, and fresh-baked bread with all its reasonably priced entrees.

You may recall from a previous chapter that I once tried a thirty-year-old homicide case where the defendant was arrested by federal marshals in Brooklyn, New York. When I subpoenaed these marshals, I received a letter from the U.S. Attorney's Office in Newark informing me that under the applicable provisions of the U.S. Code, the government would be moving to quash my subpoena. It also instructed me to contact them regarding the matter.

I arranged a meeting at the U.S. Attorney's Office, and since it was in Newark, I asked one of my foodie detective friends, MCS Detective Mike Graham, to come along. For years, I had regaled Mike with stories about the food at these restaurants, and he did not hesitate for a second when I asked him to drive me to the meeting. Newark is about a two-hour drive from Atlantic City.

During the meeting, the assistant U.S. attorney (AUSA) explained to me that it was necessary to inquire about the anticipated testimony of the marshals so as not to compromise any ongoing or future investigations. When I explained to him that their testimony would only encompass circumstances surrounding the defendant's arrest, he said there would be no objection to having them testify.

He also told me the brief meeting could have been accomplished over the phone. That way, we would not have to have driven for two hours. I told him had I done that I would not be able to have lunch in Iron Bound. He smiled and then asked Mike about his involvement in the case. When I told him Mike was not involved at all, but was only there for lunch, he asked Mike, "First time?" Mike told him it was, and the AUSA said, "You are going to love it."

Mike and I enjoyed a great meal, and he has been back to Newark many times since. While the job certainly had its downsides, it absolutely had its rewards too.

A HOUSE DIVIDED

FOR MOST OF MY CAREER, the office was like a family. Of course, there were times that it was dysfunctional, though for the greater part the staff usually participated in putting the "fun" into its dysfunctionality. The office was non-union for the attorneys working there as assistant prosecutors during my first twenty years. We were "at will" employees, meaning that we served at the pleasure of the county prosecutor and could be terminated without cause.

Salary negotiations for us were non-existent. Each year, the prosecutor determined what salary increases, if any, his attorneys received. The clerical staff were unionized, all investigators who were not superior officers were represented by the local police benevolent association, and the superior officers who were investigators negotiated directly with the prosecutor on their salary increases. When the contract employees and the superior officers were finished with their negotiations and the county signed off, the assistant prosecutors were left with whatever scraps fell from the table. Additionally, all the organized employees could only be terminated "for cause."

Before I continue, let me say that I was always treated fairly by the prosecutor when it came to annual raises. Many of my colleagues did not fare as well, and most assistant prosecutors assigned to the Investigations Section financially benefited solely from working in that section. I personally feel that the prosecutor had a greater affinity for that part of the office because most of his career was spent working there before he became county prosecutor.

I could have been a part of the inner circle. About halfway through my career, the first assistant prosecutor approached me, saying that the prosecutor wanted me to work in the Investigations Section. To his credit, the prosecutor allowed me to choose whether I wanted to transfer from the Trial Section. Quite frankly, it would have been less work and posed a greater opportunity for promotion to chief assistant prosecutor.

At the time, I was enjoying trial work because of the variety of cases on my workload. If I accepted the transfer, I would have been pigeonholed into one of a few specialized units. I declined the transfer. Days later, when I rhetorically asked the first assistant how the county prosecutor reacted, he said, "Let me put it this way. Your stock just went way down." It took another six years and a new county prosecutor before I was promoted to chief assistant and supervisor of the Trial Section.

I worked for the same prosecutor for twenty years. It is remarkable for a county prosecutor in New Jersey to serve so many terms, which speaks volumes about the job he did in maintaining a professional, career-oriented office. Like all things, however, nothing lasts forever.

When it became clear that he would not be appointed to another term, a group of quick-thinking assistant prosecutors felt this was a crucial time to organize. Without the protection of "for cause," a new county prosecutor could "clean house" by terminating any current assistant prosecutors.

The group chose the right union. The president of the union was a powerful woman who happened to be dating the governor at the time. All that was required to adopt the union were the signatures of the majority of assistant prosecutors on union cards. Adoption would not be easy. As I described, the office was divided between the Investigations and Litigation (which included Trial) Sections. Almost half the attorneys were faring well without a union.

Two of my best friends in the office, Dan Murray and Jack Lipari, helped spearhead the union movement. They came to me and said the vote was close, but if I signed a union card, other assistant prosecutors who feared that getting involved would cost them their jobs would be swayed to sign. I asked them if I could think about it overnight. A final organizational meeting was scheduled for the next day.

I fully supported unionizing, but feared an office that was already becoming divided would be split even further apart. I especially wanted to discuss it with my wife, since being terminated for participating was a possibility. I was only two years away from being able to retire. Foregoing my pension and being unemployed would have been catastrophic for us.

My wife was aware of the financial inequities in the office and gave me her wholehearted support to join the union despite potential consequences. When I attended the meeting the next day, I was still a bit apprehensive. That is, until one of the chief assistant prosecutors from the Investigations Section, who I felt was there to derail the meeting, looked squarely at me and said, "Some of you have been treated very well by the prosecutor." I looked her in the eye, said, "Give me the fucking card," and signed it under her nose.

The remaining reluctant assistant prosecutors followed me in signing the union cards. The union was officially approved, and the next year or so proved to be unpleasant.

The prosecutor froze our already approved raises for that year, but after a year of litigation, the union successfully won them back for us. Additionally, our friends and colleagues of twenty years, the chief assistant prosecutors in Investigations, refused to join the union, arguing that they were management. They lost that battle through litigation by the union, which demonstrated that they were not management since they had no hiring or firing capabilities. Finally, the incoming prosecutor said we would get "for cause" over his dead body. He did not die, and we got "for cause" as part of our first contract.

The contract established a salary scale that rewarded experience gained through years of service and was based on job responsibilities. The union also preserved our special part of the state pension system. This special part allowed us better retirement opportunities than the state system, something that the new governor had vowed to abolish as part of his campaign rhetoric.

Unionizing tremendously benefited those assistant prosecutors whose hard work and dedication went unrecognized for too long. It also fractured many friendships that were formed over years of working together. Overall, much was gained and lost, but change was necessary.

ONE OF A KIND

HOPEFULLY, WE ALL HAVE MET great people in our lives. By great, I am not talking about someone who has achieved significant wealth or notoriety. When I talk about greatness, I am speaking about the kind of person who you admire for their consistent courage, compassion, and commitment to doing what is right. The kind of person who brings a smile to your face every time you think of them. While I met many good people during my career as a prosecutor, my late friend and colleague Dan Murray stands out as great.

Dan grew up on Chicago's north side. He attended Catholic schools, was a huge fan of all Chicago teams (a much bigger Cubbies than White Sox fan), an Army veteran, a high school English teacher before going to law school, and somewhat of a perfectionist. Dan was a man of many talents and interests. He was brutally honest, non-pretentious, fiercely competitive, a creature of habit, an impeccable dresser, and both physically and mentally tough. Now that you have been introduced to Dan, let me share stories about him that incorporate most if not all his traits.

Before I joined the office, Dan worked alongside the head of the Investigations Section. He must have been impressed with Dan's work, because once he became the county prosecutor, he assigned Dan to supervise the Narcotics Unit within the office. This was one of the most prestigious and difficult assignments a prosecutor could have. Among Dan's duties, he was responsible for overseeing the county detectives and officers from other police departments who were assigned to the County Narcotics Task Force (CNTF).

The purpose of the CNTF was to investigate and prosecute major narcotics crime within the county. While Atlantic City has a population of approximately 38,000 people, some 27 million visitors each year are drawn to its casino gambling and nightlife. Unfortunately, where you find people looking to gamble and party, you are going to find illegal drugs. Additionally, many low-income people live in the shadows of the casinos, and those neighborhoods suffer from high crime rates, including drug crimes.

The reader might think Dan's job was simple, since finding narcotics traffickers in Atlantic City must be as easy as spitting into the ocean from the beach. It was the volume of cases and accountability for them that made his job difficult. Most of the detectives assigned to CNTF worked undercover. In the simplest terms, their duties included identifying drug dealers—usually through information provided by confidential informants (CIs) or making controlled purchases of drugs through CIs or undercover purchases themselves—and working their way up the ladder to the larger drug dealers.

Most purchases were made with "confidential funds" appropriated in the office budget. Once enough information was gathered to establish sufficient probable cause, these officers would prepare a search warrant that would be presented to Dan for approval. I cannot tell you the number of times I heard CNTF detectives grumble about having to rewrite a search warrant to correct grammatical or spelling errors, no doubt a result of Dan's past as an English teacher and his constant strive for perfection. Normally, when the warrants were signed by a judge and then executed, CNTF detectives found substantial amounts of drugs and cash.

The drugs had to be precisely inventoried because the quantity of drugs determined the seriousness of the crime charged. The cash also had to be precisely inventoried since the office would ask that it be forfeited as proceeds of the crime in court. The number of cases made with Dan at the helm was astounding. As a result, CNTF detectives encountered many unsavory characters, and copious amounts of drugs and cash. It is important to rotate these detectives often because burnout is great, and temptation always looms.

When Dan began to discover a pattern of misuse of confidential funds, he went to the prosecutor to discuss it. As the story goes, the prosecutor was furious at Dan for insinuating detectives would misuse the monies, and Dan was removed as supervisor of the CNTF and the Narcotics Unit. While he remained in the Investigations Section, Dan was assigned menial tasks much beneath his expertise. Yet he stayed loyal and committed to the office. Years later, a detective was fired and charged with misuse.

Dan was an avid birdwatcher, and like everything else he did, he devoted himself to it. I first became aware of Dan's passion for this activity on a drive back to the office from lunch one day. As I am driving, Dan starts shouting, "Stop, stop! Didn't you see that?" Fearing that I had run over something or someone, I immediately pulled over to the side, asking, "What, what?" Dan said, "About twenty yards into the woods. Don't you see it?" We were surrounded by woods, so it was like asking me if I saw a drop of water in the ocean.

He then pointed out exactly where I should be looking and described a bird foraging on the ground that my untrained eye would have never seen. Dan then began to regale me with the bird's migratory habits and how unusual it was to see it this far onshore. The knowledge he possessed about this small bird was fascinating, and it was astonishing that he saw it from a moving vehicle at that distance.

Dan was also extremely interested in trains and train lines, both passenger and freight. In fact, he authored a book about trains. Like all things he did, Dan thoroughly researched what he wrote about, acquiring and retaining a plethora of knowledge on the subject. I was in his office one day and he had several photographs on his desk that he was examining. One of the photographs he had was of an old roundhouse located in my hometown of North Tonawanda, New York. I was familiar with the structure and had passed by it hundreds of times growing up. It was a cylindrical tower-like building that had been boarded up for years. Now, it was as though I had seen the small bird in the woods. Dan was excited when I told him how I was able to identify the structure. For the next twenty minutes or so he taught me the history of the building and the railroad line it was on.

Dan was given the nickname "tough guy" by one of the characters we worked with after an incident that occurred at the local university. The county prosecutor, who I am sure chose to avoid the event himself, sent Dan as a last-minute replacement to an on-campus event involving NORML (National Organization for the Repeal of Marijuana Laws). At the time, New Jersey had not yet legalized marijuana.

As you can imagine, Dan was not well-received by the students in attendance. In fact, he was so heckled by one of the students that Dan said to him, "Hey tough guy, you want to go out in the parking lot and settle this?" Much to the chagrin of the county prosecutor, the incident was front page news in the next day's local paper. Members of the public criticized Dan's actions in letters to the editor, and he was reprimanded for his actions.

What the public never knew was that, months before, as Dan was driving home from a high school mock trial practice where he volunteered for years as an attorney coach, he came across a uniformed police officer being attacked by three men. This occurred in the same town as many of the shootings I describe in this book took place. It was also in the same community where Dan formerly taught high school English. Without regard for his own safety, he stopped, got out of the car, and joined in the fray. Two of the assailants ran away and the officer, with Dan's assistance, was able to arrest the third.

Dan wasn't a big guy. He was of average height, and I can only describe him as a wiry Irishman.

Dan was always impeccably dressed. He owned more starched white shirts than anyone else I knew. He was also a creature of habit. Dan ate lunch at the food court in a local mall every day, and always had the same thing: sushi. Going to lunch with Dan was like stopping for a beer with Norm on the television show *Cheers*. Everyone in the place greeted him, and the owner always gave him something new to try for free. He always brushed and flossed his teeth after lunch.

Dan was the only person I have ever known that never had a cavity. In fact, he worked out regularly, did not drink or smoke, and never gained a pound in the twenty years I knew him. He played ice hockey in a "no check" league and he "jacked up" one or more players in the locker room who didn't honor that rule.

Although Dan sometimes had a short fuse, he was truly a compassionate person. He was the first person to congratulate you in triumph and to lift you up in defeat. He was generous with his time and his treasure. When someone in the office suffered the loss of a family member, Dan was the first to offer his condolences and to ensure that all the prosecutors anted up on the collection taken for them.

Everyone who knew Dan was shocked to hear news that he had an inoperable cancerous tumor on his kidney that was spreading to other organs. When Dan was admitted to Sloan Kettering, it was time for a group of us to make a road trip to New York. We knew the prognosis was not good. In fact, when we met Dan, he told us that he had six months to live if he remained in the hospital and began chemotherapy. If he declined that treatment, it would be a matter of weeks before he passed.

Dan initially said he did not want chemotherapy because all it would do was prolong the inevitable. Collectively, we told him that the six months would allow him to spend time with his children and grandchildren, and we could help with arranging for his wife to receive his pension insurance. Dan opted for the treatment, and while the next month was a living hell for him, he was discharged from the hospital within a month in good spirits.

A couple of weeks later he called me while he and his grandchildren were driving to one of his favorite places, the upper peninsula of Michigan, to spend some time together. Dan asked me for a few "knock, knock" jokes he could tell the grandkids to pass the time as he drove.

A month or two after that, Dan and his wife, our friend Larry and his wife, and my wife and I went out to dinner. Dan insisted on driving us all in the vehicle he had just purchased. It was a vehicle he had wanted for some time. We had a great evening, and everyone was in terrific spirits.

Two weeks later, I got a call from Dan's wife that he was in the hospital and dying. As she tearfully explained to me what was happening, I could hear Dan telling her not to tell Larry or me to come to the hospital because he did not "want us to remember him that way." He passed away an hour or so later. You were a tough guy to the very end, Dan. Rest in peace. I will never forget you, my friend.

MAKING FRIENDS FOR LIFE

THE FIRST TIME I MET Rose Riddick, conditions were less than ideal. Her oldest son Carmen had been murdered just days before, and she confronted me at the killer's initial court appearance with a petition containing several hundred signatures. The petition called for me to be removed as prosecutor on the case because I and the office were racist. You might wonder how she, her family, and other members of the community reached that conclusion without ever having met me before. Let me explain the circumstances as they existed, as I explained them to Rose.

Around the time that Rose's son was murdered, there was another murder in the county. In that case, a white man of some means who owned a construction company, shotgunned his white girlfriend to death in one of the casino employee parking lots as she was about to report for her shift as a cocktail server. That defendant's bail was set at $2 million. Rose's son was African American, and his killer's bail was set at $250,000 full cash. Rose, her family, and the people who signed the petition calling for my removal, felt that the $250,000 bail requested by the prosecutor's office was disproportionately low compared to the $2 million bail on the other case, and was only requested because the victim in the other case was white and her son was black.

I explained to her, and the other members of her family who were present, that the purpose of bail is to ensure a defendant's presence at future court proceedings. Also, that the owner of the construction company had the ability to post a higher bail necessitating the $2 million figure, while her son's killer, who had just been paroled from a prison sentence he was serving in New York, was extremely unlikely to post $250,000 cash. I emphasized that setting bail had nothing to do with a victim's race.

I told them, as I did family members in every homicide case, that I hoped never to be in the same situation as them—having to place confidence in a total stranger to obtain justice after losing a loved one. Also, if at any point in the litigation they began to lose faith in me, they could request that another prosecutor be assigned to the case. If they stayed with me, however, I would use every bit of my experience and effort to ensure that justice was done. Finally, I told the Riddick family that it would be a long journey, and we would be seeing a lot of each other before it was over.

The last time I saw Rose was years later when she had passed away. We became exceptionally good friends in between our first meeting and her passing. A lot happened during that period to cement our friendship.

Carmen Riddick was murdered on his forty-first birthday.

That night, Carmen, his common-law wife, his dad Charlie, Rose, and Carmen's siblings got together at a local restaurant to celebrate his birthday. Carmen had three young children, and the children were being babysat that evening by his wife's sister. When the celebration ended, Carmen and his wife went to retrieve their children. His wife's sister and her boyfriend lived a short distance from the restaurant. Also staying at the residence was her boyfriend's brother, who had been paroled just a month before from a New York prison after serving a sentence for attempted murder.

On the drive over, Carmen and his wife got into an argument, and by the time they reached the sister's apartment, his wife decided she was going to spend the night there with the children. The argument had spilled over onto the front steps of the sister's dwelling, and words were exchanged between Carmen, the sister's boyfriend, and his brother. Eventually, Carmen decided to go home and to pick up his wife and children in the morning.

When Carmen got home, he called his own brother and told him what had occurred at his wife's sister's place. He said he was going to spend the night at home and return in the morning for his wife and children. After that conversation, Carmen's wife called, apologizing for the earlier argument, and asking him to come get her and the children. Carmen agreed to get them, not knowing that the drive over would be the last moments of his life.

The sister's boyfriend and his brother, who were irritated by their earlier encounter with Carmen, were lying in wait for him. He arrived at the sister's home, climbed the two stairs leading to a small porch area, and was ringing the doorbell when the two men attacked him. Carmen was a good-sized man, and although he was knocked to the ground, he eventually began to get the better of the sister's boyfriend. That is, until the boyfriend's brother stabbed Carmen in the back with a large knife he'd taken from the kitchen.

The knife pierced Carmen's pericardial sac, which surrounds the heart and allows it to beat within the chest cavity. When the pericardial sac is pierced, it fills with blood from the chest cavity, and the heart, having no room, stops beating. Carmen died within minutes.

Carmen may have survived if someone present had immediately called for emergency medical services. But it was dark on the side of the building where the stabbing occurred, and since only the boyfriend's brother knew about the knife, everyone else thought Carmen was lying there recovering from the fight. One of the first officers on the scene had known Carmen for most of his life. He was a physically and mentally strong detective whom I had known for most of my career. I will always remember how other officers at the scene told me that upon finding Carmen, the detective openly wept.

The defendant was arrested hours later, and although detectives searched the apartment, the knife used was never found. However, they did notice that a large knife was missing from a butcher block set in the kitchen. During the year or so that the case wound its way through the system, I got to know the Riddick family well because they appeared at many status conferences and the final pretrial conference, at which a date was given for trial. These dates are used for plea negotiations and the exchange of discovery, which includes witness statements, crime scene and autopsy photos, the medical examiner's autopsy report, and any other miscellaneous information associated with the case. What I discovered for myself was that the anger I witnessed the first time I met with the family was not motivated by grief alone, but also the guilt they had surrounding Carmen's death.

As you may recall, they were out celebrating Carmen's forty-first birthday. They had planned a celebration for his fortieth, but Charlie had been admitted to the hospital that day, and the celebration was cancelled. The first wave of guilt came with asking: "If we had been able to celebrate last year, maybe this might have never happened to Carmen." His brother was left wondering: "If I had only gone to see Carmen after our phone call, maybe he would not have gone back to the apartment for his wife and children." Carmen's wife's guilt stemmed from her feeling that, "If I hadn't argued with him, decided to spend the night at my sister's, and then called him to come get us, he would still be alive." I spent the year constantly reassuring them that the only person responsible for Carmen's death was the defendant.

The judge assigned to the case was a member of the subset I previously referred to as excellent. He demanded that attorneys appearing in his courtroom be prepared and professional, which included always being respectful to the court. It was not the first homicide case I had tried with him. In a previous case that lasted weeks, there was one occasion when I failed to stand up to raise an objection, and he reminded me in front of the jury that he "did not entertain objections from seated counsel." Despite his authoritarian approach, I enjoyed trying cases with him because you were forced to bring your "A" game.

All trials have memorable moments, and this trial was no exception. The first moment came during the testimony of Carmen's wife's sister, who was testifying for the prosecution. During her direct examination, she started talking about photographs that she was shown by a detective who interviewed her in preparation for trial.

My detective and I had interviewed her during trial prep, but we never showed her any photographs. This was a red flag. Defense counsel had hired a recently retired detective from the prosecutor's office to help him in preparing his case. I cannot be certain, but from my prior experience, this witness may have thought she was speaking to a detective from the prosecutor's office. The prosecution cannot tell a witness to refrain from speaking with the defense. However, there is no ethics violation in the prosecutor telling witnesses that any inconsistent statement they give can be used to impeach their trial testimony.

That warning usually has a chilling effect on defense interviews. She later explained that during the interview she was shown the photos to get her to change her testimony so that it was more favorable to the defendant. The defense has a reciprocal discovery obligation not as broad as that of the prosecution, but any statement made by a prosecution witness during a defense interview should normally be provided to the prosecution prior to trial. While I felt I had been "low balled," I shrugged it off because it did not really hurt the case. My detective, however, took umbrage with what had happened, and during the next recess, I had to get between him and the defense investigator to avoid fisticuffs in the courthouse corridor.

The next incident took place after a particularly long day in the trial's second week. The normal trial day started at 9 a.m. sharp. There was usually a ten-minute midmorning break, a one-hour break for lunch at 12:30 p.m., a ten-minute midafternoon break, and then trial would recess for the day at 4:30 p.m. As we neared the end of the day, I began thinking about soccer practice that evening. At the time, I was coaching my son's Under 13 travel team, and we were preparing for a big game on Sunday that would decide the championship. It was 4:20 when I had finished my direct examination of the prosecution witness, and when the judge asked defense counsel how long his cross-examination would take, he replied, "Ten minutes at most."

He droned on and on for the next forty minutes, asking the same questions over and over. I could have objected that his questions were asked and answered, but often if the objection is overruled, it just encourages a defense attorney to continue droning. Also, the jurors were beginning to squirm in their seats, which is an indication that they also had heard enough, and the line of questioning was going nowhere.

At ten minutes after five, I decided to grant myself and the jury a reprieve. I rose to my feet and objected. The judge overruled my objection, and realizing that defense counsel would now feel empowered, I briefly shook my head. The judge was upset. He ordered me to sidebar, threw a Xeroxed copy of a case at me, and told me if I did not like his ruling, I should read it because the case supported it. The jury appeared shocked by his behavior, and the Riddick family, who were sitting in the gallery directly behind where I sat, were shuddering.

I gave the judge a minute or so to cool off, then told him loudly enough for the jury to hear that I wasn't shaking my head over his ruling, but rather because defense counsel, who had said he would take ten minutes, was now an hour into his cross-examination. The prosecution traditionally sits closest to the jury because it has the burden of proof. This particular courtroom was situated such that I was right next to the jury, the spectators in the gallery sat right over my shoulder, and the judge sat on the raised bench furthest from me. When I got back to my seat, I turned to the Riddicks, who were still quite shaken, and told them in a tone of voice which may have been loud enough for the jury (but not the judge) to hear, not to worry because I had spent plenty of hours in the principal's office when I was a kid. The jurors' smiles told me that I had scored bonus points. Those points doubled when the judge next announced we were adjourning for the day.

Defense counsel's cross-examination was a prelude to his summation, which droned on for two and a half hours. I once read an article written by professional jury consultants, which concluded that a jury focuses on counsels' argument for twenty minutes before delving off into sexual thoughts, often about fellow jurors. The first twenty minutes of my summation was spent refuting the defendant's self-defense/defense of others defense.

When both summations ended, the judge spent two

more hours reading the legally required final jury instructions on the law. It has been my experience that no matter what the defense and prosecution argued, and despite the judge's instructions to the contrary, the jury has often made up its collective mind by the time deliberations begin.

During my twenty-five-year career, I had over two hundred jury trials. Lengthy jury deliberations usually meant one of two things: a majority of jurors were trying to convince a small number of holdouts to vote one way or another; or the jury could end up hung (deadlocked), in which case a mistrial would be declared, and the prosecutor would then need to decide whether to retry the case. Considering that the trial lasted two weeks, and the summations and jury instructions took six hours, the jury verdict in this case was rendered very quickly—within an hour.

Most defense counsel will tell you that a swift verdict means that jurors have found the defendant "guilty as hell." On the other hand, prosecutors will tell you that a swift verdict means the jurors rejected any evidence and any arguments made by them. The time between the sheriff's officer telling the judge that the jury has reached a verdict and gathering everyone in the court room to receive the verdict can take up to thirty minutes.

I can honestly tell you that on all two hundred plus occasions while waiting for the verdict to be read, I went from an adrenaline rush to feeling as though I was going to vomit all over counsel table. The more serious the case, the stronger the rush and feeling. It is the best and the worst thirty minutes of a prosecutor's life.

Whenever a murder verdict is rendered—and no matter how few people attend the trial—any attorneys who are in the courthouse, all the courthouse staff, and supporters of either the defendant or the victim fill the courtroom. The defendant is brought in by sheriff's officers, his shackles are removed prior to the jury entering, and several officers surround the prosecutor for protection and the defendant to dissuade him from attacking his lawyer or the prosecutor. The jurors solemnly file in and take their seats. The judge announces, "Members of the jury, I understand that you have reached a verdict," and then asks the defendant to rise and the foreperson to read the verdict. It's just like movies and television!

1 have kept you in suspense long enough. The jury found the defendant guilty on all counts in the murder of Carmen Riddick. The jury filed out, and the judge, as is done in all cases when a guilty verdict is rendered, asked, "Prosecutor, do you have any applications on behalf of the State?" I responded with my favorite words as a prosecutor, "Your Honor, with its guilty verdict the jury has stripped the defendant of the presumption of innocence, and since now more than ever he poses a great risk of flight, the State moves to revoke his bail." The judge revoked the defendant's bail, set a sentencing date, and the defendant was reshackled and escorted out of the courtroom.

With those words and actions, the Riddick family saw the jail house doors slam shut on the person solely responsible for Carmen's death. Rose was the first person to greet me. She had tears in her eyes—as did all the family, me included—gave me a hug, and asked God to bless me. Right after that, the Riddick family and I shared a group hug. I then explained to them that at sentencing they would be allowed to speak and express their feelings about how much Carmen meant to them, and how terribly affected they were by his death. We exchanged one last hug. I said I would contact them shortly before sentencing, which was scheduled in a month.

I had worked hard on preparing and trying Carmen's killer. In fact, it had consumed most of my waking moments for the month leading up to trial, especially during the two plus weeks of testimony. Trial preparation does not end once the trial begins. A prosecutor should never be myopic about a case and should strive to improve and adjust the presentation as it progresses to maximize the impact the evidence has on the jury. This, as you can well imagine, leads to little sleep while the trial is underway. In addition to sleep deprivation, a trial drains you emotionally. Especially in a case like this, where the victim's family are wonderful people hanging their expectations of justice on you.

The jury verdict came in shortly after lunch, and by the time my detective and I were leaving the courthouse, it was three in the afternoon. "Let's get a drink," I said, and we drove a few minutes to the prosecutors' watering hole. There is a feeling a prosecutor gets after a trial like this ends. I can only describe it as "vacant." Giving a victim's family "closure" is the best a prosecutor can do, and in this case, I thought "closure" was bullshit. There was only one thing that would ease the Riddick family's pain, and that was to have Carmen back. It was something no one on this Earth could give them. The one drink we stopped for led to more. We left the bar around eleven, and as mentally and emotionally drained as I was, I felt stone cold sober.

My wife was always a great sounding board in serious cases. She helped me immensely in prosecuting Carmen's killer by listening to and critiquing my presentation, usually around the dinner table. She knew I was passionate about this case and fond of the victim's family, and she decided to attend sentencing. That wasn't something she ordinarily did.

The courtroom was packed with family, friends, and coworkers of the Riddicks on the day of sentencing, and it was heart wrenching. Rose spoke, some of Carmen's siblings spoke, and the last person to speak about how much he meant to them was Carmen's eight-year-old daughter. She read a beautifully prepared letter she wrote to her dad in Heaven, telling him how much she loved him and missed his braiding her hair for school and making her favorite "pancakes" for breakfast. The judge was very moved by her letter, and commented on how proud her father would be hearing her words. When it was time for the defendant's allocution (statement before sentencing), he turned, faced the family, and said, "Suck my fucking dick, at least my kids can visit me in prison. You have to go to the cemetery." It was the most vile thing I had heard in my entire career.

The courtroom erupted. Family and friends tried to get over the railing separating them from the defendant, and I was pushing them back in their seats as the sheriff's officers interceded to restore order. The courtroom was cleared, and it was twenty minutes or so before anyone was allowed back in for sentencing to conclude. The defendant's previous convictions, his acts during the killing, and his disgusting words just a few minutes before, reaffirmed for the judge that a lengthy prison sentence was appropriate. He sentenced the defendant to a term of years that guaranteed he would never again breathe free air outside prison walls. Later that evening, my wife asked me if what transpired in the courtroom was unusual, and I assured her it was.

Carmen was murdered on his birthday, November 1st. In my Catholic religion that is the Feast of All Saints Day. Each year following his death, the Riddick family would celebrate his birthday at their home with family, friends, and neighbors. Rose invited me to the birthday celebration in the months following the trial.

When I arrived, some of the other guests were out in the front yard. The neighborhood was predominantly black and as I—a white male—walked up to the house like I was invited, one of the other guests stopped me to ask what I wanted there. At that point, Rose came out, took me by the arm and said, "He's my friend." We dined on chicken and Rose's fabulous homemade mac and cheese, drank a few beers, and sang Happy Birthday to Carmen. It was a wonderful evening.

I thanked Rose and told her how much I appreciated being invited, but this case so tugged at my heart that I had to move on to do justice for other families similarly situated. She understood, gave me a hug, and thanked me again.

After that night, I would on occasion stop by their home to chat. Every November 1st for the next eight years or so, Rose would call me to sing "I just called to say I love you." If I wasn't there, she would sing to my voicemail.

A few years after that, Rose became ill and went to live in a skilled nursing facility. She had lost her eyesight, and when I would visit and she heard my voice, she would beckon me to her bedside. We would talk about our children, and she would also tell me how well her grandchildren—Carmen's children—were doing. In her voice, I could tell how much she missed Carmen. Our visits would end with her telling me she would pray for me and me telling her that I would pray for her.

When Rose passed, I went to her viewing, arriving early to pay my respects. She had been through a lot health wise in the years before her death, and she looked at peace. My faith helped me believe she was with her beloved son Carmen. On the way out of the church, I was met by Charlie and the other immediate family members who were arriving for the funeral. They were smiling as they embraced me saying, "Mom would be so happy you came. You meant so much to her." With tears welling up in my eyes, I told them how much she and they meant to me.

Twenty-three years have passed since that initial meeting with Rose and the Riddick family. To this day, I remember them in my prayers. We have all come a long way on our journey.

IT WASN'T ALL SHITS AND GIGGLES

YOU MAY WONDER HOW A person can be constantly surrounded by evil while facing the unpredictability of a trial's outcome, and not be affected mentally. The truth is they cannot. Depression and anxiety are quite common among people working in the criminal justice system. Post-traumatic stress disorder lives on in the minds of many of us.

Depression and anxiety go hand in hand, typically starting with sleep deprivation. The onset of these two mental illnesses leaves you hoping that you are only suffering from chronic fatigue syndrome. Serious weight loss, a total lack of appetite, an absence of joy, and social awkwardness follow. Your ability to make decisions is so compromised that even if you could eat, there is no reason to dine out because you are unable to choose between items on a menu. These symptoms usually lead to the next phase where you become agoraphobic.

While your mind constantly races, you perseverate on a single catastrophic thought, and catastrophizing dominates your thought processes. Your coping skills seem to no longer exist. A sense of hopelessness is only exceeded by a sense of self-worthlessness, and you become your own worst enemy.

It does not matter how mentally strong you were before the onset of these symptoms. Depression and anxiety seem to weigh more heavily on a previously strong person who slips deeper into a depressive state every time a family member or friend says, "This is not you. Snap out of it." Those family members and friends love you and are only trying to help. You feel worse because you love them and wish you could make them feel better by "snapping out of it." Unfortunately, it is not that simple, and you now add your inability to snap out of it to your list of failures.

My bout with depression and anxiety came about fifteen years into my career as a prosecutor. It lasted almost two years. The love and support of my wife and family along with the understanding of loyal friends and colleagues helped me through this extremely dark and difficult period. I am grateful for the skilled mental health professionals who gave me tools to overcome these terrible beasts.

It takes every ounce of your personal strength to overcome and prevent recurring feelings of depression and anxiety. An effective technique I was given required me to break my day down into five-minute segments. Those five-minute segments then became an hour, an hour became a day, a day became a week, and so on.

If you have never suffered from the abject despair associated with depression and anxiety, I hope you never do. The only "good" that came of it for me was an understanding of how important it is to embrace the present. There is nothing we can do to change the past, and our future is not guaranteed.

Additionally, my personal experience helped me recognize early symptoms in colleagues and encourage them to seek help before their illnesses progressed. Helping others was cathartic and helped me overcome an unnecessary shame that is part of both illnesses.

I saw depression and anxiety affect people at all levels of the criminal justice system. As progressive as New Jersey purports to be, it was years before programs were created to help people maintain good mental health while working in the criminal justice system.

Mental illness not rising to the level of a defense also came to be addressed by the criminal justice system in the years just before I retired. Drug court, MICA (mentally ill and chemically addicted), and diversion programs for veterans were established and immediately proved to be more effective in reducing recidivism than incarcerating defendants.

It took a while for many of us as prosecutors to accept the utility of these programs, but proof came in the form of their efficacy. Some defendants needed to be removed from society for as long as possible. Others needed a chance to become a part of society again. The true challenge for a prosecutor was determining which defendants belonged where.

CAMARADERIE

I ONCE READ A BOOK written by a former United States senator attributing society's divisiveness to the near extinction of bowling leagues in America. Having been raised in a blue-collar community of approximately 32,000 people that previously supported five separate bowling alleys, each with leagues occupying them five nights a week, I understood his theory. The bowling leagues provided a place where hard-working people could socialize, have a few beers, and discuss and often resolve their differences. Bowling nights provided camaraderie, and I fear that camaraderie has been replaced by tribalism.

In a previous chapter, I discussed how unionizing caused a divide in the Prosecutor's Office. For most of my career, the assistant prosecutors were a tight-knit group, and although there were a handful who cared only about themselves, most of us worked together to preserve the integrity of the office while pursuing just results. The office was a place where you could commiserate with colleagues to resolve personal problems, not exacerbate them.

As we and our children grew older, family financial responsibilities became greater. The focus on making more money drove a wedge between us. While we never had an office bowling league, we could have used one to continue the keen sense of camaraderie we once shared.

Money alone did not destroy our wonderful sense of comradery. There were at least three other things that changed the office dynamic. My belief is that none of the three single-handedly drove us apart, but taken together, they all contributed to a breakdown in camaraderie and morale.

The county paid us bi-monthly. Every payday was a celebration, and religiously, most of the staff headed to the local watering hole just a stone's throw from the office. The place was fantastic. It was very local and casual, but not enough to be a "dive." The happy hour drink prices were great, and the food was good. It provided a wonderful place to congregate and blow off steam.

When office disputes fueled by a few cocktails became heated, someone else would always step in to cool things off. The dueling parties would normally end up shaking hands and buying each other a drink. In that way, problems were never allowed to fester. How about that? Negotiation and peaceful settlement being a way to resolve disagreements among lawyers working toward the same goal.

I remember an extraordinary day spent at that bar many years ago. We were all dismissed around noon because a winter storm was predicted to dump two feet of snow on the area.

Capitalizing on the early dismissal, most of the office headed to the watering hole. Two inches of snow causes South Jersey to panic. Two feet of snow is Snowmageddon! When I left the still-crowded bar around seven, there was a foot of snow on the roads, and it was still falling. Fortunately, there were few vehicles on the roads, and the day's partying made driving only somewhat treacherous.

There were many moments of triumph celebrated and sorrows drowned at the office watering hole. The important thing was these times were spent with supportive colleagues who knew and shared the pressures of the job. When the place burned to the ground in a fire, a big part of the office camaraderie was left in the ashes.

The office did participate in a county employees coed slo-pitch softball league. Most county departments were represented including the highways, probation, and business departments. It was competitive, but not to the point where anyone risked injury for the sake of winning.

After games, the teams would get together and share a few beers. Most spouses and kids came to the games, which were played in a county park with terrific playgrounds. Meeting fellow county employees provided a shared sense of pride and camaraderie in our collective jobs. A few years later, the league was disbanded, and we had no other choice but to join a casino league whose teams had much younger players. As injuries began to mount when the league became more competitive than fun, the office team disbanded. A huge part of our camaraderie was lost, lending truth to the former Senator's theory.

Finally, and most importantly, what contributed to poor

morale and the demise of camaraderie was office turnover. Many of the prosecutors I worked with were also career prosecutors dedicated to honing their professional skills and mentoring the young and less-experienced ones. All the career people were excellent criminal lawyers. At one time, the office was one of the most prestigious in New Jersey, and a place recent law school graduates wanted to work.

Nothing lasts forever, and prosecutors' offices statewide have become a revolving door where young lawyers gain minimal trial advocacy skills before heading out to higher paying jobs in private practice. I understand the desire to improve personal financial gain, but transience undermines the consistency and professionalism necessary to maintain the integrity of the criminal justice system.

Sadly, what these young attorneys never experienced in their short stints as prosecutors was establishing and realizing a sense of camaraderie.

CHANGE

MANY PSYCHOLOGICAL STUDIES INDICATE CHANGE is one of the top five things people fear most. Whether it is perceived as good or bad, change creates much angst. When after twenty-five years, the county prosecutor was not being reappointed, much anxiety was felt among the prosecutors who remained. I did not feel any angst, and in fact, welcomed the change.

The county prosecutor in New Jersey is a constitutional officer. To become county prosecutor, you must first be nominated by your local state senator, clear the Senate Judiciary Committee, and then receive a majority vote from the full State Senate. It is a powerful position where you make more enemies than friends, and persons coveting that position often wait in hope that you screw up.

The incoming county prosecutor was a former colleague and friend who many of us had worked with in the office years before. His reputation as a trial lawyer was solid, he was extremely bright, demanded professionalism, and was bringing a new sense of fairness in making personnel decisions that affected the attorneys. Some of the staff had grown too comfortable with the status quo, and this was more change than they could handle.

I very vividly recall my friend's swearing in ceremony. His friend and former colleague, who happened to be a New Jersey State Supreme Court Justice, administered the oath of office. He also told a story I will never forget.

He talked about a man who owned an old donkey. The man was riding the donkey to town where he planned to sell the animal. On the road he encountered another man who scolded him saying, "How selfish of you to ride upon that poor old donkey. Climb down at once." Feeling ashamed, the man dismounted the donkey and began leading it by a rope as he continued his journey. The man encountered a second person a few miles later.

That person told him, "How foolish of you to be walking when you could be riding the donkey." The man, feeling foolish, climbed back on the donkey and continued his trip. As he neared his destination, he needed to cross a narrow bridge over a river.

He now encountered a third person who said, "How thoughtless of you to be riding that old donkey over this narrow bridge." Feeling thoughtless, the man put the donkey on his back and began to carry the donkey over the bridge. About halfway across, the weight of the donkey was too much for the man to bare and he dropped the donkey off the bridge and into the river. The donkey drowned.

The Justice concluded saying, "The moral of the story

being that if you try to please everyone, you will lose your ass."
It was sage advice.

My friend told me before he was sworn in that I could choose whatever position I wanted within the office except for first assistant. While it was a job I coveted, I was aware that there were political considerations that kept that position beyond my reach. My friend also told me he hoped I would choose to supervise the Homicide Unit.

He seemed disappointed when I chose to supervise the Trial Section, but promoted me to Chief Assistant, and gave me that position. He did make clear that he wanted his younger assistants to try more cases. The dynamic that changed most since he previously worked in the office was a reluctance on the part of young prosecutors, rather than an enthusiasm, to try cases.

I headed a two-person trial team for years prior and was often paired with younger, inexperienced prosecutors. My door was always open. I tried as best I could to share the experience and knowledge acquired in trying over two hundred cases, not only with my partners, but with anyone who came seeking help.

Trying a first criminal case as a prosecutor is analogous to skydiving. Although you may have received in-class instruction, there is nothing that can prepare you for jumping out of the plane and freefalling to Earth at an uncontrollable speed. The act itself requires confidence, and the only outcome that matters is landing safely. Style and added confidence come with making more jumps.

I would never go skydiving, but early in my career, I did

try my first case. I therefore knew how difficult trying a case could be for someone who had never done it. In the last five years before retiring, I conducted training sessions aimed at reducing the learning curve for less experienced prosecutors. Some took to it very well. Others had to be pushed out the plane door.

The outgoing prosecutor had an uncanny ability to keep the criminal judges at arm's length while running his office. He demanded professionalism from his assistant prosecutors, including being respectful to judges during court appearances. He always did, however, have your back in the event a judge treated you unfairly, and never hesitated to appeal a judge whose legal ruling affected a just outcome in a case. He was not well-liked by most judges, but he was respected.

When my friend became prosecutor, he attempted to approach most judges in the same way. Unlike his predecessor, he believed that some of them were his ally. One judge was particularly critical of my friend. The prosecutor spends little or no time in the courthouse because his administrative and reporting duties consume his workday. In my friend's case, he unfortunately failed to witness this judge's harsh comments about him and assumed the judge was a trusted friend.

Things got off to a rocky start for the new county prosecutor. Like most of his predecessors, and those who succeeded him, my friend was not shy about publicity. Shortly after he took office, there was a homicide committed in one of the more affluent communities in the county. The victim was a doctor's wife who was a local celebrity of sorts, and because of a stormy relationship and pending divorce, the doctor became the prime suspect. She was found in her home shot in the face. With Philadelphia major news station cameras rolling, my friend boldly announced that the case would be solved, and the perpetrator would be in custody within a week.

Hubris got the best of him; it's never wise to make such a prediction. No matter how open and shut a case may look, there is no telling what course it might take during investigation. The doctor retained the services of a high-powered South Jersey attorney early in the investigation. In fact, he was the same attorney I tried the arson case against. The doctor was also targeted in an ongoing national prescription fraud investigation. As it turns out, the doctor was arrested years later. He hung himself in jail prior to going to trial, and the person the doctor allegedly hired to kill his wife was convicted after a trial. The case became the subject of several national television documentaries.

My friend made a second mistake early on when a prominent community figure was alleged to have been involved in a highly political case. When a local reporter questioned him about the case, he responded that it was the former county prosecutor and not him who had indicted the case. The case was in fact indicted on his watch, and I surmise his predecessor may have left it for him because of its political sensitivity. It was a bad misspeak in the sense that it suggested a lack of awareness of what was going on in the office.

There was a major narcotics operation going on in the county at the time my friend assumed office. It was conducted by several agencies, not including the prosecutor's office. When my friend became aware of this investigation, he called one of the lead detectives in and "lit him up" about conducting an operation in his jurisdiction without his knowledge and approval. While I understood his consternation as county prosecutor, his approach could have been more diplomatic. I first heard of this incident years later during a conversation at the gym with an officer who was involved in the operation.

Within the first few months of his term as county prosecutor, he was summoned to Trenton for a meeting. When a county prosecutor is commanded to appear in the State capital, the meeting is most likely with the attorney general, the governor, or even both. It usually does not spell good news. My friend looked like he had seen a ghost when I saw him after that meeting. His complexion was gray, and his eyes were fixed in a vacant stare. I seriously worried that he was having a stroke. He could never reveal who he met with or what transpired during the meeting, and I knew better than to even ask.

It did not take long for the dissenters in the office to start grumbling. I genuinely believe that many people suffered from Stockholm Syndrome contracted under the former county prosecutor. My friend strove to create a greater level of professionalism, and many of the staff were not having it. Their resistance to change was apparent.

Early in my friend's term, an anonymous letter falsely accusing him of racism and misogyny was sent to the attorney general. Rumors abounded as to who sent the letter. Accusing the sender without proof would be as despicable as the sender's letter itself. I will not go there.

I found myself defending my friend not only to my colleagues in the office, but also from attacks by attorneys at the courthouse. On one occasion, I became involved in a heated discussion with a defense attorney who I always felt possessed more form than substance. The discussion was over a change to an attorney general guideline, which he was confident my friend would interpret to allow more lenient plea offers to defendants charged with certain crimes. I told him that my friend would never interpret the guideline that way. I was defending my friend's integrity and pointing out defense counsel's lack of understanding.

My friend summoned me to his office later that day. He began by telling me that, despite our friendship, he would not tolerate me publicly criticizing him. When I asked him what he was talking about, he said he received a call from someone at the courthouse who told him I was "bad mouthing" him. My earlier discussion that day with defense counsel gave me a good idea of who was behind the call. It was not him, but someone I respected even less than him.

I told my friend to get that person on the phone "right now" so I could personally confront them over their allegation. He declined, which served to convince me of who it was. What proceeded was a heated argument between my friend and me. I felt more betrayed than him since I had been privately defending him against personal attacks for months, both in the office and at the courthouse.

I had not been feeling well for a few days prior to this encounter. That night I was admitted to the hospital with a TIA (Transient ischemic attack), a precursor to a stroke. The next three days were spent in the hospital lowering my blood pressure. I underwent numerous tests. The hospital stay provided me time to reflect on my career and convinced me to retire not a day past twenty-five years.

My friend served a single term as Prosecutor and went back to his lucrative private criminal practice. A short time later he became seriously ill, and not long after that he became bedridden. We spoke frequently on the phone, and it was my understanding he did not wish to be seen in his rapidly deteriorating condition. This was confirmed by my pastor, who in administering last rites, delivered a personal message to him for me.

I was honored when my friend's wife asked me to do the Scripture readings at his funeral. It was a sad and well-attended event. Those who were conspicuously absent were people that lacked the courage to confront him to his face. Although on occasion we disagreed, I always admired his professional skills, and the strength he showed both as county prosecutor, and during the last months of his life. I am eternally grateful of our friendship. Rest in peace, my friend.

WASN'T THAT A PARTY?

MY LAST DAY IN THE office was bittersweet. I knew it would be emotional, and when three of my good friends came to me to plan a retirement party, I told them I would like to wait at least a month to allow my emotions to subside. It was a good decision on my part.

As I walked through the office that morning, exchanging handshakes and hugs with my fellow prosecutors, secretaries, the gals from the Victim/Witness Unit, custodial staff, and detectives (including the great men and women in Homicide), my emotions gushed, and tears streamed down my cheeks. In the end, paraphernalia collected from my office fit into two cardboard boxes. The memories I acquired could fill a warehouse.

Honestly, when I walked out the office door for the last time, I felt like a tremendous weight had been lifted from my shoulders. At the same time, my heart was heavy having to say goodbye to friends and colleagues, many of whom meant the world to me.

My good friends Danielle Buckley, Lynn Heyer, and Bruce DeShields organized my retirement party. Danielle and Lynn were my "lunch wenches," a name they coined and were proud of. It derived from the three of us eating lunch together most days at the Special Services School in the same complex as the prosecutor's office and courthouse. You met my good friend Bruce in a previous chapter.

I chose to have the party at an American Legion Hall in a local community. That venue was chosen because it was a nice, casual place, and the last thing I wanted was something pretentious or stuffy. I met with a gentleman at the hall to reserve it. He asked me how many people might attend, I asked what the building capacity was, he said 185 people, and I said that would not be a problem. Over 200 guests attended.

I also asked if we could bring in our own kegged beer because the Legion only served one brand, and I wanted to give those in attendance a choice. He said that would be no problem, but by law, anything left in the two half kegs needed to remain on the premises. I told him that would be no problem at all.

The party was catered by a local barbeque restaurant, and for the $35 price of admission, each attendee enjoyed a buffet, which included chicken, ribs, sensational jalapeño mac-n-cheese, green beans, and corn bread. It was all-you-can-eat, as well as all the wine or beer you could drink, plus dancing. The music was provided by a DJ friend of mine, and the dance floor was lively throughout the evening. Additionally, a cash bar was available to guests preferring to drink something else.

Having to leave any remaining keg beer never became an

issue. Both kegs were empty two hours into the party. One of
the bartenders that evening was a retired police officer I knew
well. He said because I was a veteran, the hall could provide
bottled beer for the Legion price of a $1.50 per bottle. Bruce
told me the bar tab came to a little over $3,000. Everyone in
attendance had an enjoyable time. Me included.

I was honored to have my wife, Denise; our two adult
children Jennifer and Christian; my future daughter-in-law
Kim; my mother-in-law, brother-in-law and his wife, friends,
neighbors; office coworkers; courthouse staff; public defenders, other defense counsel; and police officers I had worked
cases with over the years in attendance.

My best friend from law school, Lorraine Stanley; my
childhood friend Lee Rynkowski and his lovely wife, Sue; my
longtime friend and dentist, Steve Katz; our dear friends from
North Jersey and the BIMOS crew (so named because we
would get together bi-monthly), Roy and Claude Lundgren,
Arnie and Rosemary Edelstein, John and Holly Hayes, and
Al and Mary Rooney were among those who made the trip.
I rented a jitney, which is a twelve-passenger bus to chauffeur
my family and out of town guests to the party. The driver also
took us to the after party and back to where everyone was
staying. This allowed us to pregame it a bit because we had a
designated driver.

Two of the judges, who were my friends, spoke. Jim Isman
was the first to speak, and he recalled one of the many cases
I prosecuted in his court room. In that case, defense counsel
filed specious motion after specious motion, which tied us up
for a month's worth of Friday afternoons. Every one of his

motions was denied and his client pled guilty. On the day of sentencing, when he had the audacity to seek a lesser sentence, the proceeding got contentious. This lawyer was from Philadelphia, looked like Pat Boone, and always wore expensive (thousand dollar plus) suits.

As Jim recalled, we had taken a necessary break in chambers to confer, but really to calm things down. While we were all walking back to the courtroom, Jim remembered me saying in a loud voice, "Hey Judge, who 'da thought we'd see Pat Boone today?" He was wearing what looked like white or tan buck shoes that did not compliment his fancy expensive suit. Years later, I saw that lawyer again when he represented the former President at his impeachment trial. He hadn't changed.

Al Garofolo spoke next. He started me off on my career as a prosecutor when he hired me twenty-five years before. I tried several cases in Al's courtroom, and he said kind things about me. One of those our daughter will always remember. He referred to me as the Clint Eastwood of prosecutors.

The current county prosecutor, my lunch wench and friend Danielle, and Bruce also spoke. Bruce was then in charge of Homicide, and on behalf of the unit, presented me with a nice set of poker chips that comes in its own engraved silver carrying case. My wife and her bowling team, "The Ballbusters," serenaded me with a special song they had composed for the occasion. Those gals contributed greatly to the festive atmosphere.

I made it a point to visit every table and personally thank each guest for being there. Despite what that sage old lawyer told me many years before about the hatred that comes with being a prosecutor, I felt loved. There wasn't a person in that room who hadn't contributed to my career through either their encouragement or providing a listening ear when I needed it. In the case of the police officers, their dedication and professionalism led to many successful prosecutions.

We wrapped things up at the American Legion around eleven thirty. About eighty of the partygoers went to the pre-planned after-party at a local bar. The revelry there continued until around two thirty. It must have been three thirty by the time the jitney driver finished dropping everyone else off and brought our daughter, my wife, and me home.

I really didn't need it, but poured myself a couple fingers of Irish whiskey and went out on the back deck. As I stood staring at a starlit sky, I thought how lucky I am to have known so many good people in my life.

While many days had seemed long, my years as a prosecutor passed quickly.

ACKNOWLEDGEMENTS

First, thank you to my family and all my friends who encouraged me to go forward in capturing these thoughts. Also, many thanks to my editor Hart Cauchy and Team Leader Zinzi Robles from Mission Point Press for their professional skills, which guided me through the process.

Finally, special thanks to Jeff Krull who inspired and mentored me — a chance meeting has turned into a good friendship — and to my friend Sue Rynkowski whose feedback was most helpful in shaping the early raw material.

ABOUT THE AUTHOR

Chet Wiech is a retired Chief Assistant Prosecutor from Atlantic County, New Jersey. With a career spanning twenty-five years, he advanced from presenting cases to grand juries to supervising all trial attorneys.

Throughout his tenure, Wiech conducted over two hundred jury trials, including twenty high-stakes homicide cases, tackling nearly every offense in the New Jersey criminal statutes.

After retiring in 2013 and placing his law license in retired status, Wiech continued to serve his community as a school security officer for three years. For the past thirteen years, he has passionately volunteered as a tutor and tutor trainer for Cape Atlantic Literacy Volunteers and New Jersey Literacy, where he successfully prepared countless immigrants for their citizenship tests.